Mama at her granddaughter Karen's wedding in 1980, age 70.

My Mama Said...

Wit, Humor and Reflections from an Extraordinary Depression-Era Woman

Compiled by
Lee Easton, Jr.

HERITAGE BOOKS
2007

HERITAGE BOOKS
AN IMPRINT OF HERITAGE BOOKS, INC.

Books, CDs, and more—Worldwide

For our listing of thousands of titles see our website
at
www.HeritageBooks.com

Published 2007 by
HERITAGE BOOKS, INC.
Publishing Division
65 East Main Street
Westminster, Maryland 21157-5026

Copyright © 2003 Lee Easton, Jr.

All rights reserved. No part of this book may be reproduced or transmitted in any form or by any means, electronic or mechanical, including photocopying, recording or by any information storage and retrieval system without written permission from the author, except for the inclusion of brief quotations in a review.

International Standard Book Number: 978-0-7884-2485-8

Dedication

"My Mama Said..." is affectionately dedicated to:

Patricia Wingfield McCormick-Goodhart

She helped my mama through her most difficult time...when she was dying of cancer. Patricia was one of the three people who started The Hospice of the Piedmont in Charlottesville, Virginia. Patricia said that my Mama was her surrogate mother...I think my Mama was surrogate to a lot of people.

TABLE OF CONTENTS

For the Reader	vii
Introduction	ix
Chapter One	
Family	1
Chapter Two	
Love	11
Chapter Three	
Religion	21
Chapter Four	
Observations	33
Chapter Five	
Humor	67
Chapter Six	
Potpourri	81
Chapter Seven	
Childhood	89

For the Reader...

My mama wrote every day, several times a day with her fifty-pound reporter's dinosaur typewriter. At least ninety-nine percent of what is written here were witticisms and occurrences that she experienced. You may come across one or two things that seem familiar or that you may think came from someone else. I, as the author apologize for that. My mama was unique in many ways and I am sure that you will enjoy what she has written...

I used that same typewriter to copy from her original papers. I hope some of her spirit remains to satisfy the reader.

Lee Easton, Jr.

INTRODUCTION

My mama's name was Evelyn Bridges Walke Easton. She was a formidable woman, tall and pretty, and she carried herself proudly which garnered respect from most of the people who knew her. She was a very good mama and I don't think I was ever able to "put anything over" on her. She was smart as a whip and had an excellent sense of humor.

She loved all four of us in different ways. She knew when we were sad or lonely inside ourselves and knew how to bring us out of our sadness. She knew the things that made us happy and was always able to get us to laugh along with her. She knew when we were having a hard time in school without us ever having to say so. She told us she loved us every day even though she didn't have to because she showed us she loved us in many different ways. She would do little things for us that let us know she loved us. Sometimes she would sit with us on our breezy front porch and tell us about when she was a "little girl." We heard all about the places she would go and things she would do when she was younger. She had been raised in Richmond, Virginia, her birthplace, and would tell us about the times that she would rollerskate in Monroe Park, or about the times she would be taken to Virginia Beach to play in the surf, or about anything she thought would be of interest to us as children.

She taught each of us to read before we went to school. She would tell us of the importance of being able to read and spell and because of her, I never misspelled a word all the way through my school years. In fact, when I was out on my own in college or when I was in the United States Air Force, people would learn that they could skip using the dictionary by just asking Lee how words were spelled.

We were all born in or just a little after the Great Depression on the late '20's and early '30's. I can remember hobos coming to our house, (which must have been marked by them), and asking for some work to do so they could buy food. They were not drinking like some of the people who approach you on the street nowadays, but were sincere about their needs. Mama

My Mama Said...

would give them some menial task to accomplish and by the time they were finished the work assigned, mama had a meal ready for them, often a hot meal. I remember I asked her once why she fed other people when we were probably as poor as they were. I remember her always answer. She would quote a place in the Bible that said "you never know when you might be entertaining an angel, unaware that they are an angel", to put it in her words.

I was small for my age and had sicknesses when I was young such as what they then called "yellow jaundice", and had a badly broken arm which healed a little crooked. I can remember my mama pulling me in a Radio Flyer wagon all the way to town and back to see various doctors. The hospital was two miles away from our house. There was no bus and taxi rides cost too much, so away we would go in our wagon for the ride. Mama worried about all of us as we were growing up. Many times she went without so we could have the bare things of necessity. She had two "wash dresses" and one good Sunday dress and said she didn't require more. She had two pairs of shoes, one brown and one black. She said they were sensible shoes, (they didn't have high heels).

Mama made sure we all had a good protestant religious education. We ALWAYS went to Sunday School and church every week, walking, of course, even though we did have an uncle who would come and get us sometimes and bring us home. He had a 1929 Hupmobile which was a pretty blue car with dark green upholstery and shades that pulled down on each of the side windows.

Mama's husband, our daddy Claude, left us when I was seventeen and mama took in boarders. They were from the Virginia Workshop For The Blind. A few of them were also deaf, which meant they were blind, deaf and couldn't speak. I learned sign language from them and was able to carry on a conversation with them and we spent many hours on our nice front porch, sitting in rocking chairs and "signing" back and forth. One of the blind boarders, Raymond Rayley, enjoyed keeping our furnace going. He would stoke it every night with the coal that would be delivered through a one foot square door with shovels into a small part of our unfinished basement. Recently a small boy who visits

My Mama Said...

his father next door asked me what that small door was and I told him it was a coal door. His retort was, "What's coal." Small children have a way of making you feel very old.

My mama loved children. There were many of them in our neighborhood and we were especially friendly with the Lang family who lived behind us. Their house faced onto the next block. Mrs. Lang had seven children. My sister was friends with Coty who was also interested in the fact that mama could play the piano. Mama played as good as a concert pianist and though she played "by ear" she encouraged Coty to take piano lessons and today Coty plays classical music and performs in yearly recitals. Coty has told me often that the reason she plays piano is because mama got her interested when she was a little girl. Coty and her sister Florence were a lot of company and good friends always.

Hunter Lang and I were same age friends. We would pretend to drive cars, running through the neighborhood with many car noises of motors and brakes. I remember that once Hunter had taken four cigarettes from his fathers cigarette pack and came over to our house and said in a low voice that he had the cigarettes and we could go out behind our chicken house and smoke them. I had never smoked, still don't at seventy-two years old, but I tried that day.

We went behind our chicken house and sat down by the fence and lit a cigarette each. Well, it wasn't a picture of fashion as I sat there choking and puffing without inhaling. I saw mama stick her head around the corner of the chicken house and look at us for a moment and then her head disappeared. A few minutes later she called me and asked me to come into the house for a minute. I put the other cigarette in my pocket and went into the house. Mama said, "Do you have another of those cigarettes?" I pulled the cigarette out of my pocket and gave it to her. She took a kitchen match from the holder on the stove and struck it on the stove lid. Then she took a puff and blew it out through her nose! I thought that was the most ridiculous thing I had ever seen. Mama exclaimed, "Isn't that glamorous?" I told her what I thought and she said to me, "Son, if you are going to smoke them, you will have to buy them. Since you only get a salary of twenty-five cents

My Mama Said...

a week, how are you going to afford to smoke?" I suddenly wasn't enamored of smoking any more.

Mama was telling me that she didn't approve of smoking, and since I have lost many friends because of the smoking habit it is another time that mama was right. Mama also didn't drink alcohol and disapproved of those who did. I remember that each time we were sitting and rocking on our front porch and mama saw someone coming down the road that appeared to be staggering, she would get up and go into the house until they had passed by. I bartended at clubs while I was in the Air Force to add to my income and still I don't drink alcohol. Again my mama was a good influence on my life.

Mama never learned to drive. When she wanted to make a little money, she would get on her bicycle and ride it around the neighborhood selling Avon products. She had a lot of customers, possibly fifty or more, and was always faithful to get the products they had ordered out the same day they arrived in the mail. I also remember that when the company had special, offers mama would buy a few and sell them later, after the offer was over, at the regular price.

When I was old enough to drive a car I would take mama to deliver the Avon. She always tried to pay me for the gasoline (which cost from 19.9 to 21.9 cents a gallon). I wouldn't take the money but mama would find a way to pay me by buying something for me or paying when we went to the new McDonalds restaurant.

I remember that mama got it into her head that she should buy six cemetery lots at the graveyard near Thomas Jefferson's estate, Monticello. She and I went up to the cemetery and she walked around and after a while she said, "I want these six right here." Well, they didn't look any different than any of the other gravesites so I asked her why she wanted those six right there.

She exclaimed, "You can see, the house from here." I replied that someday when we brought her up there for a funeral she wouldn't be able to see the house. Mama replied, "You can see here from the house, also." I knew what she was telling me. I often, go there and sit on the tombstone which mother picked out

My Mama Said...

because it was of a pretty rose marble, (she also picked out her casket), and think about her and the influence she had on me. I keep silk flowers there and change them seasonally. There is a Christmas bouquet of a mixture of silk poinsettias and some tree decorations from some mama liked which I put there each Christmas season. Mama has a footstone also which reads, "Father in your precious keeping, leave we now thy servant, sleeping." Mama picked out the words.

The reason this book is being written is because our mama kept a piece of stationery in this very typewriter and every time she had a thought she would go to the typewriter and type it out.

She kept a stack of "my writings" and when she died, we divided them. I have a stack of one hundred and thirty pages. I have gone through them and categorized the thoughts and sayings that she typed out and I hope she may be a small influence on your life, also...

I love my mama very much. You see, to me she is not dead, only sleeping like the verse on her footstone says. Someday she will awaken and she and I will take up the good times again...(I'm going to be in the grave next to her.)

CHAPTER ONE
FAMILY

I was astonished to find out that my babies turned out to be people.

When she sleeps all of the impishness goes out of her face, leaving it grave and sweet.

I remembered how the tousled curls of my little girl were still damp from her nap and later on I saw that hair smooth and shining under her bridal veil.

What those kids need is a good case of tired blood!

My idea of cleaning up was to empty an ash tray, pick up the Sunday papers, remove dead flowers and put the slippers in the bedroom.

I'm not a good nurse because I suffer with them.

I began to feel like the invisible man who could move about among real people and see them but couldn't make himself heard.

I never read Dr. Spock. I'm not sure he was "out" when I was having my babies but I don't believe he could have helped me. Too many facts just get me confused; I trust my own instincts.

I sympathize with the small school who said, "faith is believing what you know ain't so."

Please find my mother. She's lost.

My Mama Said...

My kids were turning that nervous corner of adolescence, growing away from me in little ways, and closer to me in larger ones.

Their voices mingled almost as if in music; the man's gentle understanding, the child's from the bottom of a small broken heart, the woman's seeming come not from her bosom but from the sloping bosom of the hillside, with love in it, and consolation, and long experience with trouble.

I felt the walls of home containing me, the atmosphere of home settling down about me as if in layers.

I was drowning and he wouldn't let me come to the surface to tell him I was drowning.

Their sweet little voices made the carols new - there seemed to be a halo over the manger that no stagehand or electrician had hung or turned on.

Christmas traditionally falls at the height of the earache season.

There are some four letter words that shock new brides - like cook, wash and iron.

I don't want them to think of their grandmother as something they go to on holidays like a museum.

I am living in a three bedlam house.

From the kitchen comes the comforting clatter of rehabilitation.

When they were babies, I was endlessly transfixed by the late show, the late, late show and even the test pattern.

My attic looks like a shipment of Care packages.

My Mama Said...

All God's creation belongs to all of God's creatures. May you think of my flower bed and know they bloom for you, my dears; may the sun that warms me shine on you, my precious children.

My first baby! I watched her for the next six days with an extravagance I could not sort out, the chief of which was amazement. Amazement that she could be so real, so alive, so perfect. Amazement that I was her mother, responsible for her, for her present and her future, and I realized that I was not just me any more but a separate person, and now I, was part of something that goes back and back, and on and on...

My recollection of kith and kinship never seems to agree with anyone else, Everyone under discussion was either very old or very dead. Any statement made by one person was always immediately challenged by several others. They take today for granted, yearn for the future and yet have no past at all.

It was only a surface sleep. I was aware of the ticking of the clock, the purring of the furnace below, 'til fingers of daylight gripped the windowsills.

She was speaking out of her vast experience, acquired in the sandbox.

I needed to share things with him, and sharing things with him seemed completely impossible.

As a housewife there is no time off, and it doesn't pay much, but the fringe benefits are wonderful.

Grief has made me impervious to any of the threats I know.

The price tag on you, I've paid it, haven't I? Do things your way, be the kind of person you want. Perhaps I've helped you,

My Mama Said...

telling you over and over how priceless and wonderful you are until you really believe it.

It's the night before Christmas, and I miss all the little creatures around the house. They had the right to go their own way. The fault was mine in trying to hold on to them. But they were like a fresh breeze - they made me feel young again, I guess.

We never get over wanting to start fresh again, take a new hold on life, look young again, until it gets to be a habit and you don't notice that the years are piling up behind you.

The house, bursting apart at the seams with children's running steps and war crys, roller skates, galoshes, sneakers clogging the doorways and front steps. Tricycles, fire trucks, wagons, crayons and toys littering tables and floors. Voices clammering to be heard. Piano practice, radios... Funny how things were so long ago. You would think some of it would have lingered but now the thunderous quiet that comes down over me can hardly be borne. The ticking of the quiet fills the kitchen now. The kitchen which used to steam with wet galoshes and dripping raincoats, spicy from the aromas...remember "french apple pies?" Remember fried chicken, Easton special salad, homemade soup, gallons of it bubbling in the big kettle? There was seldom money enough for haircuts and new shoes, or even dimes for the collection plate at church. But, you were a happy bunch!

A house should change at Christmas. The rooms spiced with pine, closets becoming enchanted lands where treasures lie hidden, but those are only outward changes. Something else must change. Something within the hearts of those within the house. It's those cards with elongated Saints on them that I can't stand. The house is decked with green and garnished insignias of the season. The wind is at the windows, the shingles whispering on the roof, the decorated windows, the first carol. We were the greatest promoters of Christmas cheer in the

My Mama Said...

county. What fun there was sleighing down the slopes of the fields. Every year it was over the river and through the woods to Evelyn's house we go, for them.

First you would put your slippers and robes on and had your breakfasts. Then you got dressed and went into the living room and admired the tree and opened your presents. Then, the big dinner! It all sounds simple now, but it was as involved as a coronation. Afterward, the cake with citron on it... also pine needles, I think. We were a chapter from Dickens, multiplied by the radio show, "One Man's Family." Anticipation is a very important part of Christmas. We look forward to it for weeks and when it is over we look back on it and remember only the good parts; it blends into a kind of nostalgia glow; candy canes, the smell of the pine and fir, the sound of carols being sung, the turkey, the glow of the lighted tree...

Little children, little people. So precious and so honest, they are like birds in the sky: uninhibited, shy, free from the fetters that bind adults. They say what they want when they want, good or bad. Their relationship to each other is completely honest.

Lee, my little boy, thin and bony; hands as thin as bird claws. His heavy new shoes looked clumsy at the end of his skinny legs. Leaving for school, he perfected the wet fish ease of escaping my embrace, but slowed once in his trajectory to wave goodbye.

My divorce... there were no formalities, no interminable meetings, phone calls or details of separation agreements. Just a paper signed; just him telling me that I'd be calling for him to come back within two weeks. The man I had been married to for twenty-one years went, no grief for the children he was leaving; or the wife. Just bemoaning the fate, of the chickens he had to sell, "just as they were about to lay." There was no court case, no judge, no questions. We signed a paper and that was that. A few seconds and twenty-one years of marriage was

My Mama Said...

over. I was keyed up; busy with details, scared. The finality of it hit me like a hammer. I know HE didn't think it was over. It all happened as suddenly as a thunderstorm. I was close to panic. It was like a recurring nightmare.

I was Mother Nature, knee deep in children; my own and other peoples. It was incessant, games and cookies for small fry.

My children were often preposterous, sometimes precarious, sometimes impossible, but always infinitely precious.

I knew myself to be a complicated machine. I was Evelyn Easton, who loved for things to happen to her; who went for books, and music, and poems and plays. Evelyn Easton, a woman of passion and passions, who had picked up a man in Covington, married him, bore his children and gotten lost. I tried to make it work. I tried to make his blood race a little, and mine too; I tried to build a flood to carry us off of the shoals back into deeper waters of marriage, and finally I hung on as a mother and homemaker with a kind of desperation as though I would be a zero without those functions.

The children, running to me with a bug or flower; someone must see it, someone must marvel as they did. Someone to share the moment with them.

There are days when kids are impossible, like Monday through Sunday, for instance.

Things seem to know when they are wanted and used. Houses, especially. The children are the blood of the house...and they run and laugh and stomp through it. When the children go one by one, the rooms die one by one. The shadows seem deeper and softer and the house is mine again and filled with serenity. Life comes softly into each room and pulses the air about me and warmth seems to linger there, and peace.

My Mama Said...

My diary is a day to day journal in which I record all the flotsam and jetsom of my life, and my genuine attempts to come to terms with the facts of my life.

Security and peace and love that is all I ever wanted from life. As long as the house was warm, and the children were there and there was plenty of food and health, I felt like I had more than most people dream of...

I wasn't born this old; I grew into it and someday they will too, and when they do, they will know this feeling I am having now, at least, I hope they will...

My children grew up with me, or I with them. Jackrocks, Parcheesi, Pollyanna, Checkers, Monopoly, singing around the piano. And oh, the Christmases! Homemade fun and recreation because we didn't have much money. But we had as much fun as people with five times the money we had. And oh, how I loved my family! Perhaps more than my children love theirs, because I never had a home and family before. This house was my first real home; these children my first family.

A woman's house is her hassle.

I guess I relinquished my life to my husband for the most impractical reasons - his smile, his deep brown eyes, his white teeth, his thick dark hair. But then, isn't all love based on such fragile beginnings? The real test lies in the practical day to day living; not only candles on a cake, and chilled soda pop, but also unmade beds, dirty dishes, sick kids. You may think I know nothing about marriage because mine fell apart. Right? Wrong; I'll tell you what I know about marriage. It is the most important thing there is. When one falls apart, it's terrible. When you have a good one, it's marvelous. Appreciate it; enjoy it; nurture it; fight for it. This is the message to each of my children.

My Mama Said...

My visions of a baby had been lace and silk and beautiful toys and furniture, but a baby was also wet diapers and colic and teething and upchucked bottles of milk. But as those little faces gazed up at me, and their little toes curled and uncurled against me, I knew that in silk or in burlap, a baby was a baby, little and helpless and wonderful and beautiful.

Remember the circle of faces around the table in a more innocent time - the family whose love had been a roof over our head and a memory which would always be. It washes over me; the smell of cedar and spice, the polished silver and the mended place on the table cover. The youngest child on two stout volumes with unshakable solidarity. I hear again the mumble grace being said, see the light in my children's eyes, and taste happiness like a morsel on my tongue.

I am trying to learn to stand alone and develop my inner resources so that when old age comes, and come it must, I can accept it with courage and a minimum of burden to those I love.

When they grow to a point where you can live with them, they decide to move out.

Some people use contraceptives at every conceivable opportunity.

I not only cook food well, I wear it beautifully.

I knew a child that fought loneliness and insecurity by striking back at everyone around her.

I swear, I have got to clean this house! Dust? Lawrence of Arabia couldn't have made it through such dust. I swear that if we came from dust and return to dust, someone is either coming or going under my bed.

How do we let them go? How do we find courage to let them ride skates and bicycles, to climb and dive and cross streets?

My Mama Said...

Some people make "housewife" sound like a disease.

Between reading, writing letters, watching TV, cooking weird dishes, phoning friends and cleaning this eight room house, who has time to be bored?

Maybe I'll have that cocktail now called "marriage - on - the - rocks."

My children needed me - now I need them.

A new family term - jubilant delinquents.

Children drifting in and out like migrating butterflies.

The future is yours, my children. I have brought you up, loved and nurtured you, battled for you and with you when necessary so that you may take my place. It is hard to not burn your fingers when you pass the torch.

I can only hope that my children will somehow realize that I have problems of identity also. For years I have been defined as a parent and now I must discover all over again who I am in relation to my grown family. I am wandering through a sort of "Alice In Wonderland," discovering that my croquet mallets have turned into flamingos.

It would be nice if kids came with knobs so we could turn down the sound.

My living room - the look of it with it's books and pictures and lamps in the twilight.

Sunshine streaming through my kitchen window; the satisfaction of growing older and realizing that I hadn't noticed it and a knowledge that the ones I love are doing exactly what they

My Mama Said...

want to do. A cup of coffee with a neighbor...a letter from one of my children.., My children! The link with the past that gives me a reason for tomorrow. My first child, the first miracle, the beginning, the Genesis. The next two, the continuance, my last child, the culmination. The first two babies sustained us through the hamburger years. Our apartment, furnished in Early Poverty; our feet, the first mode of transportation. Things got a little better and a little lighter during the lives of the second two children.

Somewhere you are going to have to give up something. If you marry and have children, you will have a more dependent life and you may feel "put upon," sometimes. But if you work all your life and never have anyone to lean on or to lean on you, you may feel equally "put upon" or unhappy. So, no matter which way you choose, you are going to lose something and gain something.

I tried to scale the wall that separated us, but it was too high; I couldn't make it. If I could see through the wall, what would I see? Won't they try just a little bit to scale it, too? Can't they see, I am older, I am alone and it is a much harder climb for me? If there is a door in this wall, I pray God that I will find it and it won't be locked.

CHAPTER TWO
LOVE

You are the wind the sunshine on my doorstep. You are Autumn somehow made human, blowing down a deserted street. We will swim and eat and lie in the sand, we will talk to the birds and look for starfish and you will find the most beautiful shells in the world. We will listen to the voice of the surf, and the cry of the gulls and each other.

I could talk to him as if I were talking to my own soul.

She was like a hummingbird, darting hear and there, seeking, seeking for something or someone to still this wild, wonderful confusion in her heart. She was so hungry – but perhaps it was good to be hungry, but oh, would she ever be filled?

With the sound of your voice, I come alive as a warm and living person, when you walk through that door, the house becomes brighter, warmer.

We made love as if it had just been discovered, and we had discovered it.

Never may the fruit of love be plucked from the bough and gathered into barrels; he that would eat of love must eat it where it hangs.

Just to say his name brings him close to me again.

In my marriage my takeoff was tops, but my landing was lousy.

Don't ever waste love; don't ever drive it away. It is too precious.

My Mama Said...

Can we ever go back to the magic we had then? Or will there be nothing but leftovers? I have spent years turning my mind and my heart away from you because I had to survive. Can I possibly turn it all on again? I had tried to leave the memory of you behind, but I had been more faithful to you then I would wish to be.

Sex is hereditary. If your parents never had it, chances are you won't either.

The language of love has many accents,

His name ran through my mind like an incantation, in a strange way I cried because I was at last free of the beloved burden I had carried for so long, the way one feels when a loved one, long ill, finally dies. No sense of relief, only a great sadness for all the dreadful waste, for all the lovely lost days.

There was such a swelling, beautiful ache filling my body that I felt I would faint from it, I considered this feeling in awed wonderment.

For a while we went on in that ambiguous fashion, love inside, friendship outside; what ever else we might be feeling inside carefully hidden and held in leash.

I was as filled with loss as once I was filled with you.

Tones of his love reached me through the web of sleep; joy and exultation; floodtides of it - singing through my blood, carrying away the worry and the weariness. And I knew how empty my bed had been.

If I didn't come to you, my heart would leave me and come to you anyway.

My Mama Said...

So confused. I should stop, but I don't want to stop and if keeping on means eternal suffering, then I guess I want to go on suffering. I tell myself it is wrong, but I don't care. Tomorrow I'll cry but not now. Now there's only now...

One of the worst things about happiness is that is that it feels like it is going to last.

The prospect of his coming to me had been more potent than his arms around me now.

I fell in love on my own time. There is a rumor to that effect.

For a while I grieved for him more fiercely than any lover in any romance. I missed him for the fond remembrances, the lovely meetings, his smile; our talks. But I missed him for a more important reason he had been the only man who could make my body achieve the act of love.

Some people regard love as something you fall into, like an open manhole. You do not.

I loved him with every bit of my heart, so now I know all there is to know about love.

Love can reach out of the past and transform the present.

A woman starved for tenderness may place undue importance on things. A man whose marriage suffers from clinical coolness may become inordinately fond of his dog, or his guns. Or his golf.

Inhibitions about casual affectionate touching can damage sexual relations, making it an abrupt separate event instead of a natural culmination. The need for embracing and kissing, for the warmth and intimacy, for reassuring words, is as natural as breathing - or it should be.

My Mama Said...

Did I do this? What does it matter who did what, and why? We both lost. Whatever happened to us happened slowly. Somewhere we lost contact; a terrible loss.

Loving is dangerous, isn't it? It makes you totally vulnerable.

The ocean's liquid moved along the beach, reaching out toward me, and I put out my fingers; our hands met and drew back into the yielding sand and the misty air.

So, they met in strange little corners of the world where no one knew them, and there was happiness in those meetings. There was a sadness also, and a fiery need to be together; the need to cling together and then part until next time. It brings it's own punishment along with it, this kind of love. But, they asked, who were they hurting if they sought consolation in being together for such a few hours? Only themselves! Yet it hurt worse not to be together at all.

Love is never a one way street.

I believe I have boxed myself into present corner with verbal and logical decisions; meanwhile I have lost some of my capacity for love, joy, wonder?

To feel again! It hurts a little but it feels good too; like your heart has been asleep and its coming alive again with little pins and needles in it.

How strong and sure were his arms, how protected they made me feel; how vital a being he was.

And inside me a woman resisting the whole bland myth was struggling wildly to get out, and the cracks beneath my seamless surface widened.

My Mama Said...

In my mind I heard the closing of a door, the turn of a key in the lock. The deep, comforting sounds of security and love, the sound of his gentle snore - a soul such as his will always keep heaven about him.

He can perceive and understand the longings of my heart, and translate those almost indefinable emotions into words.

I don't have a window through which you can see into my heart, or my soul, or my conscience, so do not condemn that of which you know nothing.

If it's over lets not beat it to death.

There were times when just the sound of his voice made everything all right. We just had time to explore the outer boundarys of one another's hearts. We never got back into the depths of each other's minds and hearts - we didn't have time. No time. Dear God, no time.

But just sexual satisfaction isn't the answer either. The reality is love, and without love the act would be fruitless and animalistic; a loveless copulation, leaving you more alone than before...

I love God and I love you, and since when I die I will take your love with me, and leave mine with you, then there is nothing to be afraid of; we will never be apart. Not really; nothing can part us if we love each other.

Against the dark inside of my eyelids I can see him and remember how his smile lit up his face.

In one wonder-packed moment I knew all that he meant to me; right or wrong, sensible or stupid, I was his as long as he wanted me.

My Mama Said...

It is not easy to know where love ends and loyalty begins.

The world was no bigger than the circle of your arms, until finally life was so full it could only be measured by my heart. I looked at you and let the memory of you imprint itself into my eyeballs so that even when I closed my eyes I could see you.

Falling quietly and completely and irrevocably in love is such an aching, consuming process. Folks talk about giving themselves. Those are words for people who play at love. They are not the words of the Eves of this world who are such spendthrifts when they love.

I will always have what I had. That, no one can take away. I do not ask to live long. Only to be right in the wisdom of my experience; my hands full of the harvest of life. I would be willing to go at any time, since to me. Once and for all, happened a wonderful thing.

And now you are gone. "Not, here," whispers a dry leaf. "Not here," shrills a bird on wing. "Not here," sighs the empty house. "Only here," cries my heart, and it is a cry of anguish. Babel is in me but not a sound comes out. I am a clock ticking without hands; a camera for which there is no film. I hold myself willfully quiet, but it is a quiet without rest.

We watched a star slip from heaven in a long slow curve, and fall forever. "Make a wish, my darling," you said and we both wished on it, silently, like children.

I loved having the capacity for love: to give love and to be able to accept it too. I tried once and failed once to find someone, not just strong enough to deserve it, to earn it, match it, but to be able to accept it.

My Mama Said...

The human heart is unable to reach the truth because it is so constantly in conflict with itself.

I set love on the back of the stove to simmer a little.

I can hear you without my ears and see you with my eyes closed.

We took a walk at night, and the moon created a shining pathway all the way from heaven to our very feet.

The pressure of your arms making for me a tight, invulnerable world; heat lightning flickering through my veins; thunder in my pulses; then your first kiss like the sharp sting of rain on my lips. I opened my eyes and looked into yours and I thought, "Now I can see myself, very tiny, in your eyes. Keep me there inside your eyes - until I see you again..."

Dear God, by whose mercy we are shielded from these few hours, let no one snatch this heaven from us.

His love creeps along the edges of my mind, demanding to be heard, seen, remembered.

So much love! I have to find new ways of discharging it or it will consume me.

They went to bed, and finally to sleep...They didn't try to make love, they just loved. There is love, and there is love-making, and they are not always the same. Often they are not even connected.

We often die of thirst here at love's fountain side.

I have thought about love; that stream which is love. When you are a part it feels everything you do, and what you give is the stream flowing through you. You are a channel of love and it is effortless when you give yourself up to it. Love is the stream of

My Mama Said...

passion and compassion which feeds the whole world. We have been part of it - taken from it - given to it...

It takes two to part, just as it takes two to love.

I think I miss you most when leaves go blowing down a street, or when I see two people walking down a road, two people who might be us, that once were us.

If he hadn't come along, I might have spent my whole life- enjoying myself.

I wanted to love but I didn't know how to handle it. I was so afraid of being rejected I had to start right in by showing I didn't care whether I was wanted or not. I would have married him penniless and followed him barefoot over any burning sands he chose. The incredible sweetness of his smile was almost more than I could bear. My anguish was too deep for tears, my memory too flagrant to be denied. I felt that rejection had been the theme of my entire life. I wanted change.

Every meal shared with love is a feast.

Love is not an art to me; it is Life, and the wine of desire still runs in my veins.

He was like an oasis in the desert, but now it's over it seems more like he was a mirage.

I may not always understand you, but I will always love you, and love is more than understanding.

I saw him, the room, the white sand, the limitless ocean and the great ball of sun as if from all sides at price. It was so beautiful, so magical I feared to breathe lest I change something. Time seemed to stop and I wanted it to never start again. It was a

My Mama Said...

beautiful scene, we were part of it, and I felt an ineffable happiness.

I had the frightening feeling that unless I could find a way to bring him back we would keep drifting further apart until there was a space between us too big to bridge. For some reason he was drawing a circle around himself and pushing me out of it. "There was nothing you could do," I said to myself. "Oh, yes there was" I could have-loved him more and better. I felt like a toy he was tired of playing with.

Lose your parents, you're an orphan, lose your husband, you're a widow, lose your lover, what are you?

I'm glad he came around while I could still be salvaged.

If he loves me, he has magnificent control.

What does a woman do when she faces a world full of dreams, then loses them piece by piece?

In math we never lose ourselves, but in work, sometimes yes; and in love – always.

There was a gap between the Eve I was and the Eve I wanted to be, and he was the only man I've ever known who could close that gap.

Perhaps, some day, I will not even be able to recapture the regrets I am feeling now.

I have known the joy of belonging to him, the warmth of his presence. But now it's all gone - suddenly more gone than ever before! And I felt the panic button being pressed on each and every nerve ending.

My Mama Said...

I discovered what I was to treasure most about his lovemaking - the conversation that followed it. Here at last was communication. The nearness of someone who, if only for a moment, was completely attuned to talking and to listening - and then, perhaps, more lovemaking.

I'll let them put on my tombstone, "She was unloved to death."

Cupid loves to play with matches

I felt so dewy-eyed when he was courting me, but after we were married it became a chore. I felt that sex was just something that was expected of you, like washing the dishes. I didn't know I was supposed to love it too. It was only after the birth of the third baby that I learned to enjoy it at all. I was definitely NOT sexually precocious. Maybe it would have been better if I had been. The Kinsey report says a woman doesn't reach the peak of her sex appetite until her late twenties. To me at eighteen it was definitely a disappointment and I produced babies without producing satisfaction.

No one is ever really alone as long as there is still another person to care for and love.

CHAPTER 3
RELIGION

To pray, not for an easier life, but to be a stronger person: not for tasks equal to my powers, but powers equal to my tasks.

When I sing of "going home," I mean a gate, a door, not a terminus, not an ending, for I believe that there is more to life after what we call death.

Make your bargain with the devil; make it if you dare; but be very sure you read the contract, and understand it's terms.

God doesn't die the day we cease to believe in a personal Diety, but WE die on that day when for us life is no longer shot through with splendor beyond the reach of reason.

It is as if I was of no value to anyone. Please, Lord, make me of value to someone. I am like an empty car on an empty road, with no passengers.

In Cor 1, Chapter 13, verse 8 Paul tells us that "love knows no limits to it's endurance; no end to its - trust; no fading of its hope; That it can outlast anything and is the one thing that will stand when all else has fallen.

Not one soul has ever been born into this world without a definite purpose for being here. Each one has been chosen by our Father who created us for His own desire and need, and the great eternal divine plan for each life lies safely enfolded within our own beings and He alone can bring our lives into fulfillment.

My Mama Said...

A deep hush outside the windows slanted gentle rain and my heart was leaden and my body numb. It is never quite possible to be ready for separation. Then incredibly it happened.

Far away through the rain I heard a robin singing and he put his whole heart into his song, and all at once my crushing burden seemed lighter; I found I could raise my heart to my Creator in song just as the little robin had done. I can hear it still whenever I need faith and courage to go on.

Our bodies are the temples of the living Christ and are made up of cells, each of which is formed from Spirit, which is life. Each cell is a citizen of a where we are King; each cell responds to our every thought, and their function in life is to build as we present the pattern. We can build our habitation on a common level or erect it on a high plane. If we follow the line of least resistance and believe only the things we can see, hear, feel, taste and touch, these little cells will build all these human frailness into our habitations. But if we realize that these visible and tangible things are unstable and temporary, and if we put our faith in the visible, eternal realities, using our God-given spiritual senses - imagination, intuition, inspiration, meditation - we will find the life building forces within us reaching out into the infinite resources of God and drawing to us all the things necessary for abundant living.

God's promises are as unfailing as His sun, His tides, His seasons. Man is one personality, made up of spirit, mind and body, essentially bound together, anything that affects the spirit leaves it's effect upon the mind and body.

Jesus did not say, "blessed are the good"; what He said, in effect, was "Blessed are those who want to be good." How reassuring is the difference! Perfection is not demanded of us. We are being told that the important thing is to want very much to be good. It has always seemed to me, in reading the New Testament, that Christ was fairly lenient with recognized

My Mama Said...

sinners. The people He critized most sharply were the Pharisees who went around praying loudly to show how good they were.

I pray that strength and courage, reason and understanding may be given to me in abundance; that the good which lies in every human heart may each day be magnified and made manifest; that men may come to see more clearly not that which divides them but that which unites them. That each hour will bring us closer to a final victory not of nation over nation, but of man over his own evils and temptations and weaknesses. That the true spirit of Christianity, it's joys and beauty, it is hope and abiding faith, may live in our hearts; that the blessings of peace may be OURS, peace to build and to grow and to live in harmony and sympathy with others and to plan for the future with confidence.

I thank God for the open sky, the brown earth, the leafy tree, the golden sand, the blue water, and the stars in their courses, and for my ability to be aware of all of this. The song of birds, the butterflies, clouds and rainbows, sunlight; moonlight; firelight; Impromptu praise, an unexpected kiss. A sense of values. A sense of humor. The will to work. The talent of sharing. The love of justice. A passion for truth. The power of faith.

God gave us brilliant sunrises and sunsets, the rolling surf, the Fall foliage, the snowy mountain peaks as therapy for the oft troubled spirit.

We worry too much about the pain and evil in the world when actually we should continually be astonished by the great amount of goodness.

There was a mass exodus to the restrooms; this is a cardinal rule at all church pageants.

My Mama Said...

The "adjust or be damned" philosophy bogs me. If Christ had adjusted to the life of a carpenter, He would have been spared the cross, but He would never have been known.

The prayers mingled together and, like a thin graceful column of smoke issuing form a chimney, began their way upward.

I don't want to possess faith; I want a faith to possess me.

Do you count sheep? No, I talk to the Shepherd.

I have taken the first steps in a long journey and I cannot turn back.

I thought it would be better to be a cheerful sinner rather than a miserable saint.

I had only a shabby second to offer the Lord, it seems. But I guess He is used to that... If I can forgive God for all He has made me suffer, why shouldn't He love me too, even though I failed Him?

You have to pray the way you make love with everything you have in you.

We should not fear death, for we experience it many times and resurrection too before we're through.

I thank Thee for clean clothes, good food, scrubbed floors, a breezy front porch, green grass, fresh air and quiet.

God never meant for the church to be a refrigerator in which to preserve perishable piety, He meant it to be an incubator in which to hatch out converts.

There is a difference between knowing the Word of God and knowing the God of the Word.

My Mama Said...

People seem to think of God as a venerable bookkeeper who takes notes of everyone's good and bad deeds. Or a King of Glory ruling the universe from some golden throne. Or the God who walked in the garden in the cool of the day - a man sized God The "God who is on our side," or the God of Battles - should be dead. We are all up against it when we try to comprehend God, for we can no more delineate God than we can pour the ocean into a pint cup. If you ask people where God is, their thought goes shooting off among the stars, but it is deep down within human hearts that we really find God.

Belief is like a roadmap. Faith is taking the journey. Faith isn't a quality of mind acquired by reason and intellect. Faith is not an autonomous power that exists only because it is directed to the power of God. Faith is no competitor of grace, but sovereign grace is confirmed by faith.

Tread lightly but firmly and with confidence. The Spirit of God is all about you.

Religion should be a beautiful temple in your heart; not something you visit once a week.

We have to be of some religious persuasion so we'll know which church we're not attending.

It was God's people that the serpent bit in the wilderness; God's people with God's seal upon their foreheads and God's love overshadowing them. And there was a cure for the serpent's bite. They were to raise up a brass serpent, and whoever looked upon it would be cured. It was a serpent that bit them. It was a serpent that cured them, Instead of God taking away the thing that killed them, He exalted that thing, lifted it up, and it became their victory. The very thing that tries to defeat us can become the thing that will deliver us. There will be fiery serpents along life's way but through trust in God we can become overcome them.

My Mama Said...

Don't just speak of God, speak To Him.

Some people are so busy telling God what they want, they don't have a chance to find out what He wants.

It's the preacher's job to comfort the troubled and to trouble the comfortable; to understand those not so good at explaining, and to explain to those not good at understanding.

Faith is a leap out of total despair.

Oh, God, your sea is so vast, and my boat so small.

From the hands of the Great Creator comes the inevitable caress of Spring, bringing life, colors of the whole spectrum, and fragrance and beauty to the eager earth.

I began to find strength only when I admitted my own helplessness.

The transformation begins when you usher in the Sabbath at twilight. What a sense of power to be able to borrow a segment of time out of eternity and ask it into your home for a majestic twenty-four hours. To have the power to declare one day out of seven to be above and beyond the slavish striving for survival.

When you meet someone like Him, it makes you want to give the whole world a second chance. If I ever feel a rush of self pity, help me, Lord to resist it, for I have no wish to play the martyr.

We look up and praise You. We commit all things unto You. We thank You for the miracle of Thyself. You have said that we have not because we ask not. Lord, we ask it in the blessed name of Jesus; come into our hearts with the fullness of Thy Holy Spirit; for YOU said to ask and we would receive.

My Mama Said...

Since I received Jesus as my personal Savior I feel better when I feel bad than I did before

I received Him when I felt good. I don't know how many more years I have to live on this earth, but Dwight L. Moody once said, "someday you're going to hear that I am dead, but don't you believe a word of it I'll be more alive then than I am right now." That's how I feel. I have passed from death into life. The Bible says that it is far better to depart and be with Christ. Jesus said, "that which is flesh is flesh and that which is spirit is spirit." I know that God has not given us the spirit of fear, but the spirit of love, and power, and of a sound mind. Tonight when I pray I can say, "Fill my cup, Lord, fill it up!" For He has filled it, and "by this we will know that we have passed form death unto life because we love the brethren." I'd be afraid not to accept Jesus Christ. He has said that of those who do not receive Him, He will blot their name out of the book of Life. (Revelation chapter 3, verse 5).

So many people in this old world today are madly searching for something, and they do not even know what it is that they are looking for to satisfy them. Maybe a bigger car, or a bigger house, or a bigger bank account. One of these days we are going to lie down and leave every bit of it us. The Bible asks, "Then whose shall these things be?"

All the high and lofty places will be brought low, and if in this world only we have hope, we will be of all men, most miserable. We all have problems, but the difference is that we have Jesus to help US bear them, and solve them, and overcome them.

I felt like I'd been struck down so low no power on earth could ever, get me up again; it was like I had died and didn't even want to get up again. I asked for God's help.

My Mama Said...

All the religions in the world are man reaching toward God. Christianity is God reaching toward man.

The greatest Sequoia trees are as blades of grass to our Heavenly Father just as our feet seem like huge boulders to the insects beneath them. Magnitude is in the eye of the beholder.

Our efficiency without God's sufficiency is only a deficiency.

Then there was the Russian child who asked his mother, "Does God know we don't believe in Him?"

If what goes on in church is a sample of how the world is going to be saved, we can scarcely wonder if the world fails to be impressed! The parade of trivialities that the typical church program offers isn't related in any way to the real problems which are clawing our souls to shreds.

I will stand as tall as my faith can stretch.

The Bible is noted for it's virtues but clarity isn't always one of these.

God gives us strength of mind and spine. You don't have to look vaguely into the sky for help.

God never leads His children other than they would choose to be led if they could see the end from the beginning.

Remember this... God can give us just as much as we need! He gave manna in the wilderness. He gave them shoes that didn't wear out for forty years! He gave water from a rock! He multiplied a widow's meal and oil so it didn't run out. He made a boy's lunch feed a multitude!

When we love God we do not have to concern ourselves with trying to measure the world in terms of miles. We can

My Mama Said...

truthfully, like the song says, "it's a small world after all," and if we belong to Him we are drawn together by His love and He is always near us.

God understands us but He loves us anyway.

You cannot get religion by dialing a number on a telephone.

"Doctor, your patient is ready to be delivered," What exciting words! There is awe and wonder in birth; it's radiance is reflected in the eyes of the new mother as she views her baby with joy and love... Even so at death - though there is grief, there is also hope, for in this transfer from life to another some heavenly messenger reports to The Great Physician, "Master, your patient is ready to be delivered."

In autumn God speaks to us in flaming colors.

Pastors sometimes overlook that temporary condition known as life and see only eternity.

There's a beautiful picture in a beautiful frame, and if God takes away the frame, I still have the beautiful picture.

I see the ten Commandments as ten marble slabs. old tombstones in an old graveyard, and when one falls, all the others topple with it, like dominoes.

We are in eternal life right now and when we go on we will be that much farther along.

When you are ready to go off the edge, remember, God made the earth round, in his mercy.

Lord, help my words to be gracious and tender today for tomorrow I may have to eat them.

My Mama Said...

What you are is God's gift to you. What you make of yourself is your gift to God.

If your day is-hemmed in by prayer, it is less likely to unravel.

Life has it's own reason for being and it isn't ours to end. Life ends in death, but death isn't the end.

I almost came to hate religion, almost rejected it, though secretly quaking with fear that such rebellion would merit fiery damnation, until I received a concept of God that made possible my acceptance of a religion that was sustaining instead of being destructive and terrifying.

Often, when we want something very much we pray to God for it and when God doesn't answer as we wish we cease to pray and become angry, and the wonderful thing is that we don't know God is taking us gently by the hand and leading us away from disaster.

God will mend a broken heart if you give Him all the pieces.

Not all my sins passed before me, but as many as could find room in the parade.

I planted it on the "pray as you sow" plan.

The purpose of prayer is not to tell God what we would like Him to do for us; it should be to help discover what He would have us do and make us willing to obey His will.

Ho, everyone that thirsteth, come ye to the waters, and he that hath no money, come ye, buy and eat. (Isaiah chapter 55, verse 1.) How wonderful that God would condescend to plead with bankrupt sinners to accept His blessings of love. It is for everyone. There is only one qualifying condition - he has to be thirsty. Therefore those who are invited are the unsatisfied,

My Mama Said...

who feel a lack, a yearning. Don't you sort of get the picture of a hot desert waste, and a cool bubbling fountain?

The church bells, are they tolling in unison or competition?

I would make the same statement in the House of God that I make out under His blue sky - because that also is the House of God

I needed a personal God. What sort of God did I have?

Remember, He who is to judge us is He who made us!

The thing is to draw religion out of a man; not to pump it into him.

For thirty pieces of silver Judas sold himself, not Christ.

The Lord doesn't only want us to reform, He wants us to repent and conform. I know the values the church upholds; love, dignity, individual rights, trust - but I see too little in the way of action and results. There is a lot of hypocrisy in the church today. It should be a place for searching inquiry and for action; not the mug, self satisfied organization it seems to have become.

CHAPTER FOUR
OBSERVATIONS

The sun with all those planets revolving around it and dependent on it, can still ripen a bunch of grapes as if it had nothing to do at all.

The disappearance of the family doctor is a tragedy, bringing much of humanity to the impersonal hospitals, causing long waits for indifferent examinations by a doctor the patient has never seen before and probably will not see again. The indignities, the inefficiencies, the long waits at every visit, the crowded, shoddy facilities, the poor attitude of the clinic personnel...

I can feel the fingertips of the rain upon my face.

The mirror gave me back my face; just a standard, faintly worried, grey temple face.

Tell her heaven? I'm not sure that's so comforting anymore with all they know about space. It doesn't seem like such a peaceful place anymore. Everything's changed, even heaven.

There isn't much nourishment in echoes, in the sound of time. Can you imagine anything so brief could become so enduring?

Sometimes you feel that the sky and the water and you - are all one - that you are a part of something big and wonderful and alive.

There is not enough darkness in the world to put out the light of "one small candle". No man is so poor as not to have many small candles; remember laughter; a tree in the wind; the face

My Mama Said...

of a loved one - and when we light these, the darkness goes away.

There is something marvelously secure about being a failure.

My poems never found their way into a book but they found a way out of me.

The hardest thing to get in a hospital is information. What is happening to you and why? I was a Practical Nurse and to me they all seemed unwilling to talk to you in any detail about your illnesses or treatment; they convey an absolute minimum of information. They have no time for conversation and have little or no patience with the emotional problem of the sick. This is too bad, since nothing would contribute more to a patient's peace of mind then a frank discussion of what is wrong with him, what treatment is prescribed and what his chances for recovery are.

The leaves are all gone, the ground is covered with snow, everything outlined in black and white - technicolor all gone,

New York! Screeching to make yourself heard above the clamor of the subway - coming up for air now and then, looking through dirty windows at soot-smeared buildings and platforms and tired washed out faces, fighting their way in, fighting for their way out. Ogden Nash called it a vermivorous vault. People in New York are. a conglomerate lot, and they trust nobody. New York after sundown is pretty grim when you're alone. The touch of strange bodies in subways, faces very close. but not seeing you. New York - so dependent on dirty taxicabs with sullen or loquacious drivers. The terrible noise of the jackhammers and compressors building and destroying on a grand scale. New York - you can have it. It's not for me.

I sat there in the silent, empty room accepting rejection, for that was what it was.

My Mama Said...

I don't want to spend the rest of my life tearing myself apart for not being a Madonna.

The hospital has got files on people who haven't been born yet.

Castles in the air can be awfully lonely and awfully drafty.

Look at them. He talks to the top of her head and she answers his belt buckle.

The statue glistened in the rain; the pigeons hide under the eaves of the huge buildings. In the lonely park lonely people sit on benches, feeding the squirrels and watching other lonely people go by.

He says we don't need psychiatrists; just better bartenders; he pours the drinks, you pour your troubles out and by the end of the evening either you have the solution to your troubles, or you didn't care for one.

You can't pour a quart into a pint measure.

Sometimes a wish carries its own ironic penalty.

To stay younger eat for youth, defeat time. You would be surprised how many things you can do to forestall the penalties of living beyond childhood. A whole variety of products to be used internally and externally, guaranteed to restore the human body almost to its original state of birth. There is reindeer meat, sunflower seeds, carrot juice, Queen bee cream, yogurt, and various other products composed mostly of the vital organs of other animals who obviously hadn't lived to test their effectiveness. But it takes more than youth-dew powder base to erase the years.

My Mama Said...

A genial spring day such as this evokes nesting birds and down payments.

I throw out words the way a porcupine throws out quills, and far the same reason.

It's hard to come up with answers when you don't even know the questions. I withdraw the question.

I am the founder and the chairman of the board of the society of frightened people.

We understand with our minds. We accept with our hearts.

The longer a man is wrong, the surer he is right.

I look into the face of misfortune and I think "if I ever get used to it, I'm lost."

There are people who think the time will come when receive an answer to all their problems, all their dreams. They will not. There will be tomorrow and the day after, and a brand new set of problems - and then what?

It would be sheer conceit for me to imagine for one single minute that I could succeed where everybody else had failed so miserably. Doctors have a way of talking all around a subject so that at the end of the conversation you have just as much information as you did at the beginning.

The pauses in the music aren't the music, but they make the music what it is.

I can no more separate those two sides of my nature than I can separate the two sides of a coin; to possess one is to possess the other.

My Mama Said...

I was in that state of agitation in which you tell yourself you are very calm, when in reality you'd settle for not falling over a chair or bumping into a lamp.

Sometimes it is possible to bark up a whole forest of wrong trees.

She is like a vegetable with a heartbeat.

I can only tell you distantly the way colors are explained to the blind.

Christmas! Cabled electric stars arched overhead. The gingerbread wisemen followed a frosted cookie star across the bakery window. Santa Claus was blowing on his hands and ringing a bell outside the 5 and 10 cent store, and signs were everywhere – "Christmas Greetings", "Peace on earth", "Only _ more days until Christmas"... There were sprigs of mistletoe even in the mahogany silence of the town library and all the current magazines were alive with red and green illustrations. Christmas?

The leaves look like they have had a wonderful summer and now are wearing autumn shades with elegance and finesse.

I am a lot of things, but one thing I have always tried to be and that is honest; with others and with myself. Maybe that's the trouble. Maybe if I could have pretended a little bit about myself and with myself, I could have been a little more smug; a little more self satisfied.

I'm about as sophisticated and worldly as Alice In Wonderland.

If you are afraid of pain, you will never know the full meaning of pleasure. If you DO things you will have something, even if it is a scar, or a painful memory...

My Mama Said...

I demand the preposterous; that life shall have a meaning. I have the certainty that our existence is meaningful and therefore that life must have a purpose. To escape from the shell of ourselves we must make connections with other human beings. I have the desire to share what is on my mind and in my heart; to share completely my aims, hopes, dreams. Even my fears.

The threat is like a known step upon the stair; it is no stranger to me, but one which has come this way before and now comes again.

How unfortunate are those who are not fitted for ecstasy; how much they miss.

We are ourselves, plus our circumstances. It is what our experiences have made us, plus what we have made of our experiences. Being locked away from life, I suppose, is also a form of experience. Experience isn't always life with a capital L.

Death sweeps away beauty as well as the beast.

Personality is not a static thing; it grows and changes.

She didn't take to age any more noticeably than the ocean.

Dying, when you come down to it, is a job. It takes planning and attention, just like setting up housekeeping, or planting corn.

The rain that hadn't known how to start, didn't know how to stop either.

The only true dignity of man is his ability to despise himself.

Iron is iron until it is rust; there never was a war that was not inward; we must fight until we conquer in ourselves what causes war, though we know it not.

My Mama Said...

Time is very poorly symbolized by a kindly old gentleman with a sharp scythe...an idiot with a blunt instrument would be more suitable.

You get just as tired doing things you want to do as you get, doing the things you don't want to do.

Just about the time you reach a goal, someone moves the goalposts on you.

Drinkers, you can't drown your troubles. They are expert swimmers.

I saw a drunk weaving his car back and forth, playing what's my lane.

Sometimes silence is alive with sound.

You never find happiness by chasing it; you have to open your heart and let it happen.

At the Senior Center I met a gang of senior citizens who clearly had not led normal lives and didn't intend to start at their age.

Peace is for the old and defeated. YOU can find peace in the grave.

They work overtime to try to increase the span of man's life, and then they insist on retirement at 65. It is not only senseless, it is criminal. There are fifteen or twenty years of extra life. They are pushed out of the main stream by this society they helped to build. A number is picked out - a magic number like 65. Then hocus-pocus you're out. Fear begins at 50. It takes a lifetime to make a mature person - then we brush it aside; we put it out with the garbage or we turn it off like we would a bad TV program.

My Mama Said...

What do you do with virtuosity? Do we nurture it or do we run away and hide because of the chinks in our own armor?

That movie wasn't a release, it was an escape

It is a very delicate operation - to cut out the heart without killing the patient.

I guess time is a lifetime process, a slow assembling of it's inevitability.- It is some thing that only time can teach, and for some of us it never does.

You aren't supposed to fall into bottomless depths over things that happen. You are protective enough to make sure your bleeding wounds are camouflaged end only you are aware of the residual scar tissue.

They were shouting at each other as if they were a mile apart.

You can be deeply wounded not only by what happens to you but also by what fails to happen to you.

I simply don't belong to the NOW generation; I am hopelessly THEN.

A record player with its dangling intestinal wires is no thing of beauty, but oh, the sound is!

It's a random chaotic world, and nobody seems to be in charge.

When you are in your sixties and almost unemployable because of your age and lack training, a place where you are valued becomes a vital center in your life.

You can't defeat pain by putting it to sleep - <u>it wakes up</u>!

My Mama Said...

He has walked many roads, none of which has led to any particular place.

We are never allowed the merciful finality of a last straw.

Two of the rarest commodities we have in a hospital are peace and quiet. Two luxuries we never take for granted,

Black wool is just as warm as white.

Christmas leaves me overspent financially, physically, emotionally, sentimentally, but it is always worth it.

My daughters had wide shining eyes, freckles like little gold stars across their noses and cheekbones. They were the greatest thing since sunshine.

He wore his dark clouds like a halo.

Knowledge is taking things apart; wisdom is putting them together again.

A little pinch of today beats a pound of tomorrow.

The chains of habit are too weak to be felt until they are too strong to be broken.

Nobody is as empty as the one who is full of himself.

Modern medicine seems bent on prolonging life, of whatever meager quality, rather than slowing down the aging process. Doctors have found ways to prolong life, but what about the quality of life?

Some people think of ownership in terms of legal papers, safes, possessions on pantry shelves, in chests, trunks and boxes. I used to feel that way, too. Now I am aware of the great trees

My Mama Said...

about me, green grass, great mountains and distances, redbirds and robins and wrens which fly from the land I own to the land my neighbors own, knowing it is all their land! And I realize some day some one else will live here; my land will be their land, my house their house. But only temporarily, and under a manmade covenant... The mockingbird at night sends forth a dazzling cascade of sound, and I think - I do not own the mockingbird, but I do own his song. God said to Abraham, "all this land will I give thee." God said to Evelyn, "all you see can be yours to keep in your heart." But we can no more keep such beauty alone, than we can cage the wind. We must share it or lose it.

The teacher might have more facts than the pupil but it doesn't make him an authority.

Too many people are interested in what a man has than what he is.

I am bored with people who drop soliloquies carefully labeled "intelligence." I am tired of cynics who call themselves "realists." I am sick of people embarrassed at honesty.

Everybody has something wrong going on most of the time, and perhaps there are times when there is value in some hell-raising worry. But for the most part I think it's good to go through the motions of acting the way you'd like to feel and maybe you will feel that way eventually.

Outside there is a benison of bird song announcing to the world that the night is over; the day has returned.

My son Lee would rock tirelessly when he was little as if keeping time to an inaudible drum.

To me, having the friendship and affection of a few close friends is better than a circle of superficial acquaintances.

My Mama Said...

I will get some of the trivia out of my life, and substitute rest. I will list the situations which loosen the tensions for me and whatever they are, I will put them on my agenda regularly, and give them highest priority. I think this will be a smart investment.

The years are gone. They're not stacked in a corner somewhere, waiting to be used again.

I wonder if maybe we were once just as afraid of life before we were born as we are of death now that we are alive, only we just don't remember it.

If I were brought to trial for the crimes I have committed against myself I would be condemned to the gallows.

He tried to weave all the loose ends into a noose.

When he spoke, he said it with deadly delicacy.

Everyone from pre-school to post mortem has a right to his own opinions.

The size of a man's head, and the weight of his brain has no bearing on the quality of his mentality.

Life comes in all shapes and sizes and sometimes it hurts and sometimes it's good.

Ant - a busy insect who still finds time to go to picnics.
Bigamist - a person who has had one too many.
Snoring - sheet music.
Married man - one with both hands on the steering wheel.
Caterpillar - an upholstered worm.
Bachelor - a man who has been lucky in love.

My Mama Said...

They are the sort of people who measure a man by counting his money.

I <u>may have</u> become a senior citizen, but I <u>have</u> become a drop-out from the school of hard knocks.

I suppose all our lives are serial stories and each day brings a new installment, and no matter how bad yesterday was, who can resist tuning in on tomorrow to find out what happens next?

Remember the World War Two years? Lady riveters, ration points, war bonds, "A" gas window stickers, pride and terrible anxiety. Every aspect of life was colored in some way by the fact of national crisis but for me the real involvement was in having someone to yearn over and worry about.

Sometimes I think I feel like I was nobody way out in the middle of nowhere hanging on to nothing.

Hate is like a snake biting it's own tail.

We sometimes can't improve on saying nothing.

Pay now. Die later! It is now possible to prepare to live out our remaining years in the company of our peers, who are about to die, and slowly drowning in their own misery. A society where life is extended but the meaning of life has vanished. If we succumb to such a life, our grandchildren naturally come to know practically nothing about us. Both generations are cut off from the two way flow of communication between young and old.

In those Senior Citizen Centers and Retirement Homes, the isolation is complete and we have only the company of our peers, and drained memories of the past. Dead minds in healthy bodies.

My Mama Said...

It is not enough just to be a good listener; if we all listened we would live in a situation of universal silence.

Excuses never plowed a field!

Talk is cheap because the supply is always greater than the demand.

You don't grow old when you cease to grow. You are old.

An unfinished remark is like a time bomb. There it lies between two people, ticking, ticking...

You stand before your own conscience, and before that tribunal alone. Justice must come and it alone can determine the degree of your penalty.

The frame of mind with which you face life will determine what life does to you.

It isn't the new light we need, it's the old light lived up to. It isn't new truth we need, it's the old truths better understood.

The sky has a pre dawn glow; not light but the promise of light approaching; a wisp of breeze whispers in the maple leaves; a robin calls as though asking who else was awake and a mockingbird answers; then half a dozen sleepy birds begin to sing. The trees are still dark shadows against the horizon. Perhaps this is what it is like to be rich – to have time to watch the maple put forth leaves in May and to watch those leaves turn to gold and crimson in October; to see a snowflake and marvel at it and the endless symmetry and variety of nature. The birds are louder now; no soloists; they had become a chorus, and the day began it's own pace; the confusions of yesterday a matter of history, as each new day offers us to get on with life. The birds are singing a hallelujah chorus now, and the leaves begin to whisper their own song. Dawn is a miracle,

My Mama Said...

sweeping away the night's darkness and returning the sun to us once more. I once heard someone say that if dawn came up only once a year we would gather on hilltops to see it and to celebrate it; we would hold festivals and issue proclamations and utter prayers of thanksgiving and I guess it is true. There is a whole new day ahead; a day that never was before and I was a witness to its creation. I know now how some people feel in the morning.

It takes a long time for some folks to learn; being a part of something, for instance. But in everything they do they have to leave one part of themselves out to act as an audience.

Life isn't having it made, it's making it. Anyone unlucky to have it made becomes a spectator instead of a participant in life, so on my next birthday I don't want to feel that I have it made; I want to feel that I'd better get going because I have one less year in which to do the things and a thousand things need to be done.

I'm a regular hotbed of tranquility.

The degree of adjustment you have to make coming down from a peak usually depends on what you will miss most at the top.

She has hair like exploding tomato surprise.

Experiences have shapes but sometimes the shapes end up having no resemblance to the experience.

Freedom was born twins and the name of the other twin is Responsibility. Moreover they're Siamese. You can't have one without the other.

We're never given a title to anything, only a loan.

Grief, if allowed to run its natural course, will dissolve into sweet memories, sometimes.

My Mama Said...

The turning point in life is sometimes the rounding of a curve, but occasionally one startling moment stands out in one's memory like a bronze marker along the highway of life.

He has lots of horsepower but no horse sense.

She is a glittering palace of ice.

Maybe I'm being childish, but from where I sit I'm not the only one in the playpen.

I went through more dramatic scenes than you could uncover in six weeks of a daily soap opera.

I never got dangerously close to the real world during those two perfect weeks and I left with even less desire to know what was going on in it. But there comes a time when each of us has to go back to reality to find dust on the furniture, a bed littered with two weeks of junk mail, (and a few nice letters), and I sat down to brood over the harshness of re-entry.

By the yard, it's hard; by the inch it's a cinch.

The secrets of a night nurse! People in pain and delirium, pouring out their deepest secrets, their innermost thoughts to an anonymous priestess in white.

I love the shore. To hear the roar of the waves, to taste the salty taste on my lips, to feel the wind in my face, to have the joy of being a part of all that wildness relaxes my very soul.

He has become a bottle baby again - and is he sloshed.

If she wants to feel guilty, let her feel guilty. Some people take laxatives; others take guilt.

My Mama Said...

If you want me you'll find me in the attic - clinging to the past.

I'd rather know a few things for certain than to be sure of a lot of things that aren't so.

People sweep out the cobwebs but they don't do anything about the spiders.

I looked into the mirror and time seemed to stand still; the tired face, the grey hair, the body thickened through the years seemed to have no connection with me. Immured inside them is the pretty young girl who still lives there...with her aspirations and her dreams.

I have never developed the healthy paranoia necessary for survival in the city.

I know a stingy old man, holding back, guarding what he has because he has so little.

The world has been made very small by the dangerous miracle of flight.

Respect is in itself a cloak against suspicion.

This is a world in which those you hope to avoid arrive from every direction and those you love best depart to the other side of the world.

There is always something we want deep inside us. Sometimes we have a picture of it, sometimes we don't; but once in a lifetime, if we are lucky, we meet up with the picture inside us.

Sometimes I can make the words flow out of paper, but then when I talk I am so inept, so faltering...

My Mama Said...

I wanted it as a small child wanted the moon, and with about as much an idea of what to do with it.

I'd rather believe in something than believe in nothing and be right.

Who am I? I'm Chicken Little and the sky is about to fall. I am Cinderella and I want to know when is midnight?

Beloved, life comes up to and goes down from such times as these, and the more level the years, the higher the perfect hours.

In the early morning the ground will be planes and terraces of light and shadows, and the birds will awaken, and all the morning noises start. I will walk across little wet feelers of grass. I will find a web, spun by some busy spider, and it will be beautiful and new, and the dew will hold all the lovely colors of springtime in little rainbow drops. Much later the evening will come, the sunlight will slant obliquely through the pines, casting long shadows over the grass. The mountain night, cool and waiting, will come down and possess the darkening rocks, the blue air around me.

I'm a country girl. I want to see Indian summer in my hair, kick through the dry leaves.

The great Atlantic Ocean is change itself. The sea itself is always new.

Here before me are snapshots; some faded to the color of caramel; pasted to stiff black album pages. In those pages lies my reality.

I am finding out how the world about us can heighten and darken under a single consuming anxiety normality goes on rattling around you, but your trouble is like a goiter no one else can see.

My Mama Said...

I have found that adjectives carry a lot more meaning than verbs.

We all carry the past with us, but we don't have to let it rule our lives.

I am surrounded by stillness and space, empty space in which there is no choice but to see things as they are.

I am living in a bombed out existence.

You don't have to be in "Who's Who" to know what's what.

Oh, the slowness of the days and the swiftness of the years.

I cannot drive a car and my bike has only one speed - me.

The world is all turned around. First they invent things so you can rest a lot, and then they tell you you're in mortal danger if you do.

My thermometer goes lower and my fuel bills go higher. I'm heating in Celsius and paying in Fahrenheit.

Some days I feel like I'm just paddling to stay afloat.

Words can wound but silence can tear you apart.

I think I am studying for my finals but the word "terminal" is okay. It's not that you live, but how you live that gives quality, beauty and meaning to your life.

Why shouldn't I try? I can only fail and heaven knows I'm no stranger to failure.

With all that isn't right about it, think of all that is!

My Mama Said...

There aren't any wrinkles on my mind or my spirit.

In some ways we always stay the same. There are basic elements in the personalities of each of us that are our essence; that are us. But we can change our circumstances, our outer life.

It is mysterious, this communication of feelings through sounds heard by our ears, but than feelings can be communicated in many different ways.

I wonder if anyone ever died from loneliness? I am sure they must have wanted to.

Women are strange creatures; their bodies pay very little attention to their minds.

He was looking for the pot-of-gold, while I was looking for the rainbow.

Yesterday's truth is today's deception and today's false influence is tomorrow's revelation.

To serve humanity or to serve a human being, which is best?

You have to be a great artist to be a good mother-in-law because all history is against you.

My ideas seem to have wings but no landing gear.

She is a strange old lady with as many sides as a diamond, and you never know from day to day which side you would hit on. The whole town accepts her as one of it's eccentrics who can stand on her head in the middle of Main Street without comment.

There isn't enough money in this world to pay me for what I have suffered, or enough money to buy the happiness I have had. If I were to turn in a bill, it would read like a psalm, the way a

My Mama Said...

psalm reads of mortal agony and rejoicing. I would not remove one bit of it it's awakening to pain, to yearning, to fulfillment, to vaulting beauty. It would be impossible to pour the new Evelyn back into the old bottle. I know that everything we feel must be a part of us forever, and I am glad.

The thought of age has never troubled me or depressed me before. What is appalling is the knowledge that life holds all the tricks, including the Joker; that no matter how you play the game, you can't win.

You cannot live forever and you always wear out life long before you have exhausted it's possibilities.

You can crush me between your hands but my rosy spirit will still be free.

Sometimes my house ceases to be a refuge and becomes a prison.

It is nice to be doing something you feel is helpful in order to "grow old gracefully", I will not be content at any age to take my place in the corner and just look on. Life is meant to be lived!

The love you give away is the only love you really keep.

They've got all kinds of things to keep us living longer and longer these days, but then they don't know what to do with us.

It is foolish to warn one not to waste time. Time cannot be wasted, spent or saved! It is like warning a fish not to waste water. We have no influence at all on time. We are born in it and it surrounds us every moment. The personal tragedy, the waste, lies in what we do with ourselves, what we could do, but don't. The effort we do not make; the powers we do not use; the happiness we do not earn; the kindnesses we do not bestow.

My Mama Said...

Waste time? Let US correct ourselves. Let us say frankly, 'I am wasting ME!'

Seashells survive by not resisting the force of the sea.

I've just come through the most painful surgery in the world - having my eyes opened.

I'm not what I was but I am trying to get used to what I've become. My wild oats have turned to shredded wheat.

Culture seems to glorify youth and newness, and considers age to be only depreciation.

Maturity is rarely regarded as an asset. One wonders if the attainment of old age is worthy of the effort necessary to attain it. The only things that improve with age are whiskey and antiques.

We must make every effort to maintain good health. Nature makes no allowances for good intentions.

We should look at age not as a period of melancholy decline, but as a farther opportunity for growth!

Which do you want - dollars or hours? You've got to stop squandering all this time making money; trading your little diamond and platinum minutes for some silly nickel. That's not good business, boy.

Some people can't afford to be rich.

We were typical pioneers, living in cold walk-ups to colder rooms; having children right in the house,(no hospital except the first), noisy neighbors in other apartments in the same house; the whole bit. I was glad I had some of my ancestor pioneers blood in my veins.

My Mama Said...

The world needs to be disciplined in high chair, not electric chair.

He has eyes like two fried eggs with catsup on them.

What I used to do in one day would give Wonder Woman a hernia.

My face looks like a ten car pileup. I look like something out of "Jaws".

That Evelyn, I can't keep up with her any more. She's gone. Just a memory. The gal I look at in the mirror these days I just don't know anymore.

Failing is a part of trying. If you never try you never fail - the only ones who never fail are those who never try.

A halo is a lovely thing but you must be able to take it off now and them.

A friend? So was Caesar before he was stabbed by Brutus.

It is Spring and the sap is running for joy; the flowers are laughing as they watch all that juice and joy.

We are all strangers within the gate; within the gate of life.

I stood at the window watching a snowflake trying to make up its mind.

Your life won't be very rich if you go to your grave without any secrets locked in your heart.

It's like being in a house of mirrors. You know it's you, but it doesn't look like you.

My Mama Said...

You become trapped by your own image in the mirror and no matter how hard you try, you can't find yourself.

Out there lie all the tomorrows we must meet, all the things that are yet to be.

He is the sort of hayseed the traveling salesman wouldn't trust his daughter with.

Our town is so small that there is no village idiot. We all take turns.

A woman has no greater pleasure than to feed a hungry man and a man has no greater pleasure than to satisfy

The only things you cannot lose are the things you have lost forever.

I felt like the Captain of the Titanic during the second chorus of "Nearer My God To Thee."

I have things that don't show up in any bank book. Sunsets, friends, watching children grow. True you can't spend these things but you can't buy them either.

I'm a slow walker, but I never walk back.

The ledger of love comes up for balancing without warning at the worst darned times.

All those words are just words that cover the surface; they tell something of what you feel, but there aren't any words that tell the whole iceberg just the tip that's showing. The rest comes from inside what you see are just surface things to which you react.
The other is reaction itself.

My Mama Said...

No person is more righteous or morally severe that a person with a guilty conscience.

When the cat's away, the mouse acts like a rat!

Perhaps the truly important thing is not how to remember but how to forget.

What's the neatest trick of the week? Cutting someone's throat behind their back.

It is distinctly possible to stay too long at the fair.

I've gone through an orgy of flagellation, but I've stopped wearing monogrammed hairshirts.

I live in a glass house, honey; I never throw stones.

You are only young once, but you can stay immature indefinitely.

It would be immoral for me to do a decent thing now for the hope of a reward afterward.

Everybody thinks of changing humanity; nobody thinks of changing themselves.

It's like a stonecutter banging away at a rock a hundred times without discovering a crack - then at the hundred and first blow it splits in two parts, and you know it wasn't that particular that did it, but all that went on before.

I see myself in the mirror and I am shocked, so different I am from what I meant to be.

How can we know what genes in us combine to form the resultant personality, or what accident of chance turned the-whole course of life in weird directions?

My Mama Said...

Then there are those who stand in total repudiation of everything.

I see dead, grey faces of thousands, going to work each day, selling their souls in the marketplace.

I'm not so sure of the wonderful training they have had. I watch some doctors and think it was a case of trial and error.

Hospital food is clean, nutritious, wholesome and completely inedible. Unless your palate is calloused, don't even taste it. Just the sight of overdone beef congealed in plastic gravy can give you a relapse.

If the patient is rich he gets more and better attention. I know. I've nursed the rich and the poor. American hospitals are the most caste ridden institutions west of Bombay. The poorer patients, in semi-private rooms are "clinical material" and therefore of interest to the doctors and medical students. Nurses spend more time in record keeping than on patients. They are overworked, their hours are uncertain and much of their work is clerical and menial. As a consequence, morale is often low. Dissatisfaction among nurses is often due to the arrogance of many doctors who seem to think the greenest intern is superior to any nurse, no matter what her experience, and this attitude can be very damaging. The last thing you can expect in a hospital as a patient is rest. Someone comes in to hassle you every fifteen minutes. Temperature, blood pressure, a snip of bone marrow, oxygen therapy, a tray of revolting food, a medication or a needle - or to shave your body so the doctors can have at you in the morning, or to adjust tubes running from your incision to a gurgling pump, or other tubes dripping something into your veins. I suspect that more patients die of sheer exhaustion than anything else.

I'm going to start putting things off, starting tomorrow.

My Mama Said...

The future is not what it used to be...

Every man is guilty of all the good he didn't do.

For me there are no strangers, only friends I haven't met yet.

Always remember, it takes both sunshine and rain to make a rainbow.

If you see someone without a smile, give him one of yours.

Youth is a gift of nature; age is a work of art.

He would probably brand me a black sheep. But then, isn't their wool just as warm?

I am older, but the surf still thunders with youth, never changing.

We are <u>not</u> just poor hairless apes with overdeveloped craniums.

You cannot order your dreams to advance and retreat.

The world is full of good hearted dingbats.

I can't see why I should be on-the defensive, but all the other positions seem to be taken.

For years, I needed to know that whatever happened, someone would be there; (someone would be there.) Someone would take care of me. Later, above all, I needed to know that I could take care of myself.

If I have to lie there while death is wrung out of me cell by cell, death will be a sort of triumph.

The more we can see into ourselves, the more we can see outside ourselves.

My Mama Said...

One good thing in favor of real life - it keeps your mind off all that suffering on TV.

Full consciousness brings joy. Once you open your senses fully to something- anything a sunset, a waterfall, a flower, joy comes. But to open your senses you have to drop out of the future and the past and stay in that beautiful present. The only true reality is NOW, The past is gone. The future is not yet. Only the joyful acceptance of the eternal NOW!

Some people are on a journey which has no destination except death. They walk through a forest and they say, "How many board feet can I get out of this tree. I did well last year, this year I must do better". Always the past or the future! They are always <u>becoming</u>, they never <u>are</u>.

I would like to think that because I once lived some small boy or girl will have a happier time. Maybe it will mean that my life really mattered after. Children are our future.

Don't hang onto life too tightly; you'll squeeze all the juice out of it.

I am reaching down into the awesome beauties of creation; reaching up and out to the awesome power of the Creator! Making myself aware of the forces within me; helping myself reach up and out to the forces beyond myself.

Oh, for the autumn, when the sun will stop baking the land; when nature will dip a cloth in cool water and wash the face of the plains and mountains, and summer, the playboy of the seasons will rest, and the lazy sun will get out of bed a little late each morning and retire a little earlier each evening. The sweet, sad season of bright and clear skies and wood smoke, and the winds come strong and sharp, stripping the trees and piling leaves like bowls of cornflakes, and there is a quick shiver in

My Mama Said...

the air. The nights become quiet, the stars wink across time and eternity; and flowers stand dead in their beds, certain of resurrection in the spring. School buses with warning lights drop off pairs of feet too happy to be trusted. A wood spider shops for a new home near the oil burner. The fields are empty. It is a sad and beautiful time, the day before the long white sleep.

Must peace be only a state of suspended hostilities?

I have decided that I will not go, hat in hand, into old age, I will fight it every step of the way!

You cannot free yourself from emotional entanglements unless you know what they are all about. Only this insight can permanently extricate one form an emotional morass. Compulsive drives only contribute to compulsive problems. The important thing is what you feel rather than what you think. Insight is an indispensable tool in solving problems. It has become as a slow and emotional upheaval and as a result of much work and tears.

The best oral contraceptive is still "No."

Lent! The long period of self denial followed by a week-end of rejoicing, only now the popular thing is to avoid the denial but join in the triumph. Can there be serenity without agony, victory without a struggle? This point troubles me.

We talk of killing time, but time kills us.

Nothing fits like a glove - including gloves.

Sometimes remembering can be as vivid as the original happiness.

You can't win a game of solitaire. If you have to play it, you've lost already.

My Mama Said...

The most useless sign is the one posted at the entrance of our post office. "No dogs allowed except seeing eye dogs."

It would be nice to be able to lean back and find something more solid than air behind me.

Keep busy, keep real busy, it's a poor substitute for what's really the matter with you but it's better than nothing.

Look over your shoulder, elderly person, take a good look, because there's nothing chasing you anymore,

The ship is sinking, but I keep on working; it's the only way I know to keep my mind off drowning.

Being frightened of the future is a natural, normal function. It's how you react to it that counts. You can whine and crawl under a bed, or you can clench your fists and go on with your business.

There is nothing wrong with castles in the air unless you try to move into them.

I guess some things are like the oil business. Sometimes it is near the surface and some times you have to dig really deep, and sometimes you hit a dry well.

You can't be secure without money, but money alone is not security.

They say you never learn from your failures. That should make me quite an authority on a great many subjects.

You can't tell the depth of the well by the handle on the pump.

The same sun that melts the ice hardens the clay.

My Mama Said...

Wall to wall carpeting, wall to wall windows, back to wall financing.

Sometimes I feel like a space walker severed from his capsule.

I have found that you can go hungry on a full stomach.

There are three ingredients in life - learning, earning and yearning.

Increased communication doesn't necessarily mean increased understanding.

The only thing that fits into a pigeon hole is a pigeon.

It isn't that I've gotten brave; it's just that I've run clear out of fear. Fall is in the air and I am in a leaf-turning mood also.

Love, adventure, music, poetry; all of these make friends with both sadness and joy.

The bandit bees, stealing from the flowers...

It was a drizzly, Hitchcock sort of day you got the heart-pounding feeling of being followed. The shadows were peopled with sinister figures of my own imagining.

The self-righteous ones are usually the most unintelligent.

Everybody lives in a haunted house - memory is a haunted house, But it may also be a friendly house, yesterdays voices echo through the rooms, cheerfully telling the good news of yesterday. Yesterdays people walk the floors, warming their hands by the glow of vanished fires. It is not a strange place, but perhaps it is wise not to dwell therein too long, but you can go there and emerge feeling refreshed and somewhat less lonely than before.

My Mama Said...

Christmas is not made of gifts and tinsel and silver balls. It is made of people who love each other, and of being together.

The purest form of giving is to beg a favor from someone who loves you.

Did anyone ever die of the joy of deliverance?

Everything comes to him who waits - like grey hair, false teeth and gout.

The gap between death and life is weak, very weak; the gap between death and life is almost impregnable.

Who was it who said, "to survive is to postpone?"

It is good to have money and the things that money can buy, but it is also good to check once in a while to make sure you haven't lost the things that money can't buy. The minds of the young are uncluttered by the past, and therefore more able to accept the present.

All the success in the world doesn't mean a thing unless you have someone with which to share it.

Our youth seem to agree on the worthlessness of contemporary American Society, yet they seem to find it hard to suggest any program for it's improvement.

We have to be proud of ourselves with rights and feelings of our own. We are unique. We tell ourselves "I am the only me there is," and we must be secure in our own identity. Some day we will have to tell our children why we failed to solve all the world's problems.

My Mama Said...

It is just as hard to live with someone who never needs help as it is to live with someone who is always asking for help.

Words! Little black marks on paper, Sounds in empty air. Yet what power they have! They can make you laugh, cry, love or hate, fight or run away, heal or hurt.

The human body can't be traded in on a new model, and anyone who risks his health for the sake of sensual pleasure by drinking and smoking must lack imagination. They must be poor in spirit if they have to depend on liquor and cigarettes for sweetness and pleasure.

America's pride in her population may be compared to a cancer patients pride in his expanding tumor. We cannot find the money we need to build schools, save cities, treat sewage, clean our air, collect our trash, give health care and adequate diet to our present population.

He spends an hour in the morning and another hour in the evening boxed up in his car, to and from the city, which he visits only in order to work, and in which he works only in order to escape from the city.

Memories of straw sailor hats, of pigtails, dimpled knees and rosy cheeks, little smocked dresses, little lisping voices; little arms hugging me. These are the fragments of life that cast shadows of longest remembrance for me. There is more to be marveled at in the ordinary than in the unusual.

We have to take a long, hard look at ourselves as members of different nations, different religions, different races and of two sexes. If we could only become conscious of our deep need for each other - and on others for life - physical, emotional and spiritual, Actually we have never been lonelier as individuals; more separated from one another.

My Mama Said...

The smog, the scorched belts of asphalt, the fields and fences, the horses and cows gone bowing to the rampant commercialism which washes over the area, tearing at people, at things which dared to attempt permanence, Space - lovely view - all obliterated in the rush of the cleaning establishment, the plumbers shop on the next block; the many prefabs where the fields once stood - but memories of the old scenes survive in those of us who stayed and have withstood the self destructive growth of "civilization" and "culture." Threads of a coherent past...and even those memories are being diluted by the deluge of a "new era."

The greatest tragedies are the opportunities we lost.

In life all emotions are qualified; happiness is shadowed by remorse: pain is made bearable by the sudden perception of beauty.

Realism has replaced idealism.

People used to tell me I should publish what I wrote. But it doesn't matter to me that what I write will never be published. What matters is that I have said what I must and I have put on record some hidden part of me that I can finally see and when I see things I have written I understand myself better.

Mama at my home in 1972.

CHAPTER FIVE
HUMOR

He's so impatient, if he was in on a space project, he would take off without the rocket.

Those shoes look like they have been cobbled by an acid-head elf.

It isn't even civilized to be this happy!

Sometimes I run hard just to stay in the same place.

Somewhere along the way she picked up a few years and dropped a few scruples.

Every knot has a couple of loose ends.

Shaggy hair, fuzzy face, thick glasses, dirty shirt, mouth wide open which he promptly closed over a cigar. Oh boy, is this about to become a father?

I've seen four people who show more emotion, and they are on Mount Rushmore.

Would you care to join me in a little window jumping?

He was studying anatomy - in Braille.

I'm not implying that he doesn't have all his marbles; it's just that they seem to be arranged a little differently from other people.

I've eaten salmon until I have an overpowering urge to swim upstream.

My Mama Said...

If all the hair in Castro's beard were laid end to end, he would have a long thin beard.

If the "flat look" takes, I will have to leave the country.

I was as nervous as a bubble dancer with a slow leak.

You never see alcohol as a problem until you seize it as a solution.

Nothing works as well as the totally unexpected. Try it sometimes.

For years I have made a career out of not knowing what I was going to do.

He was as exacting as a slide rule, as meticulous as a handmade bottonhole, and about as interesting.

He was a verbal sleeping pill.

She has all the qualities for a dull life.

He speaks in italicized banalitys.

He's the only kindergarten dropout I ever knew.

She believes in "love thy neighbor", and just about anybody else who is handy.

It was the only sensible thing he had said in a long time, but I guess you can't rush these things.

Only the Statue of Liberty looks good carrying a torch.

He is as practical as a cold in the head.

There's nothing like the guillotine for giving you a split personality.

My Mama Said...

Whistling may help me get past the graveyard but it won't remove the cemetery.

I've been trying to decide whether to kick the habit or relax and enjoy it.

I've seen quite a bit of this world-and this world has seen quite a bit of me and its been a harrowing experience for both of us.

I walked in, turned on the lights, put on the teakettle, turned on the TV, lowered the shades and decided that all I needed to complete the picture was a cat or two.

I've had enough peace and quiet to open a cemetery.

When they spoke of babysitters, I envisioned flattened babies.

I have a rendezvous with debt.

The Pill – un-conceivably delicious.

My Chicken a la King tasted like it had abdicated.

I got a look at my shadow on Groundhogs Day and predicted six weeks of dieting.

Close scrutiny had made nit-pickers of them all.

He's the only person I know who speaks in capital letters.

I was holding the bedpan before me like the Magi presenting frankincense.

If you live long enough, you become old. It's terribly simple.

My Mama Said...

He stared at me with all the fascination of a scientist attempting to identify a rare specimen under a microscope.

It's been obvious for so long; it is like refusing to admit that your house is on fire.

The room was filled with a deafening silence.

It was like bones from the Master's table with a sign saying "keep out." Trouble is, some dogs can't read.

The year is over. How very strange that it should end without a sound.

That low rumble you just heard was the worm turning.

He was preoccupied. That's a polite word for being out of your mind.

I'd say that we are both suffering from a deplorable lack of curiosity.

She's so neat she puts paper under the cuckoo clock.

I went to the beauty shop got a mud pack; looked fine for two days. Then the mud pack fell off.

Don't look now but I think I have a leak in my charisma.

<u>For Sale</u> - One slightly used magic carpet.

I felt like a shuttlecock right in the middle of a badminton game.

Then there was the male robin who upon finding a brown egg in his nest asked his wife about it. She replied that she had done it for a lark.

My Mama Said...

He pumped my hand as if there was a water shortage.

I had so much egg on my face I wouldn't have to cook breakfast for a week!

Holding a conversation with him is like juggling bubbles in a hurricane.

I feel like my whole body is mad at me.

He went out in a calculated blaze of obscurity.

He has been laboring under a profound misapprehension.

For some, standing in front of the mirror is like facing a firing squad.

I'm tired in places I don't even have.

Don't just stand there - throw something!

I had a teacher who every time she turned she erased the blackboard.

Invest your money in taxes. They will always go up.

Narrow roads where two cars could just pass have been replaced by wide freeways where six or eight cars can collide all at once.

The little things...what they lack in magnitude they make up for in multitude.

I hope it achieves the failure it deserves.

He uses his words as if he has to buy each one.

My Mama Said...

I held tight to my banner but I forgot where I was marching.

He was "most likely to succeed" for ten years.

The wolf was not only at the door, it came in and had pups.

This is the drunkest room I was ever in.

What weighs a ton and has a stick in it. A hippopopsicle

My memory book has a few blank pages in it.

I sprayed it, let it dry, brushed it, and sent it to the cleaners.

At last! A movie the whole family can walk out on.

I'll bet I could have made a wig out of all the hairs I found on his coat.

He was so mad I felt I should get out of there before he bit himself and died.

I've got hang-ups everywhere but in the closet.

You don't have to hang from a tree to be a nut.

Show me a man who keeps both feet on the ground and I'll show you a man who can't get his pants off.

A nation in which white folks and black folks can band together and call themselves the Red Skins, can't be all bad.

Cheer up! I'm told that after the show they are going to have some entertainment.

When bigger mouths are made, there will be bigger feet to go into them.

My Mama Said...

My life is an open book but the pages are stuck together.

It's like the old lady who asked, "how can I tell you what I think until I hear what I say?"

At least you make the future sound like it is worth waiting for.

Confucius was a sage old blabbermouth.

I haven't a glass slipper to my name, and I'm fresh out of castles.

He's so careful, he wears seatbelts in a drive-in movie.

I'm so nervous I even have clenched hair.

Knees buckle - belt won't

She's a news addict. If she doesn't know what is going on, she gets withdrawal pains.

I don't have to go to work. I get up in the morning and there it is all around me.

He's got more layers to him than an onion.

It's like throwing a bone to a toothless tiger.

I have a body that is more of a liability than an asset.

I was just there for the preliminaries, but from the way it started out the main event must have been a doozy!

I'm like the guy who knew a little about everything, and kept on knowing more and more about less and less until he finally knew just about everything about practically nothing at all.

My Mama Said...

Some people go through life as if it were a play and they were in the balcony.

With no decisions to make, she can make no mistakes.

Weight-wise, I was not a born loser. I can gain ten pounds by just reading the cookbook. I guess some people were born to look like Twiggy and some were born to look like Queen Victoria.

A diplomat is a person who can tell you to go to hell in such a way that you will look forward to the trip.

I have a strong suspicion that you are only a figment of my imagination.

He's the sort of person who follows you into a revolving door and comes out first.

I guess the doctor cured me. Now I am trying to get over the cure.

She has a Madonna face and a stainless steel heart.

Do you eat bacon with your fingers? No, I eat the fingers separately.

In the pan there are unidentified frying objects.

I went to an art museum. I've seen better pictures on cave walls. I've seen better and happier faces on iodine bottles.

I could knock enough wind out of her to fly a kite.

I haven't gone berserk yet, but I'm working on it.

Beauty and timelessness; The land of tomorrow; never put off 'til tomorrow what you can do day after tomorrow.

My Mama Said...

The only thing self-cleaning is the cat.

I may not be over the hill, but I can sure see the top of it.

She wore them until her tutus became four-fours.

He's the kind that would send threatening Valentines.

He looks as if he has outgrown himself.

God's country - nobody else would have it,

How much did he leave when he died? All of it.

She had a heart attack at the funeral and was probably the first woman to arrive at the hospital in a hearse.

I think my bones are held together by my imagination.

One thing about the speed of light. It gets here too early in the morning.

He has a heart problem. They can't find it.

It's like trying to draw a picture by connecting the dots with half the dots missing,

One more x-ray and I'll light up in the dark.

What does it take to get their full attention? Rigor Mortis?

The golfer had socks in sets of three in case he got a hole-in-one.

A lot of thinking gets done over a cup of tea. Maybe I should get myself a larger cup.

My Mama Said...

If I kept smiling much longer the lower half of my face was going to drop off.

She has opinions and lacks the grace to keep them to herself.

Man with Volkswagen would like to meet folding girl.

I'm such a shell of my former self if you put me to your ear you will hear the ocean.

She's so British she wears tweed nightgowns.

Her voice sounds as if it were gargling with peanut butter.

I'll take things as they come if I can handle them that fast.

I worship the ground he should be under.

Insanity is hereditary. You get it from your children.

Doors are made to knock on, not knock down.

She stayed the same to the point of petrifying.

A good way to get patients out of bed is to paste the bill on the ceiling.

The most dangerous thing in the world is to try to leap a chasm in two jumps.

It's what you learn after you know it all that counts.

Diplomacy is the art of letting someone else have your way.

An honest man changes his mind often; a fool, never.

My Mama Said...

Nothing is all wrong. Even a clock that has stopped is right twice a day.

Those who think they know it all upset those of us who do.

If you're a square peg in a round hole, start whittling.

One of the best things to have up your sleeve is a funny bone.

Minds are like parachutes. They only function when they are open.

Even a turtle only moves ahead by sticking it's head out.

If at first you don't succeed, try hard not to look astonished.

Even if you're on the right track you'll get run over if you just sit there.

He is the only guy I ever saw who could get sparks out of a knife and fork.

She had the attention span of a fruit fly.

If there was a nip in the air, he'd drink it!

If I can't get by on brains, I'll get by on brass.

Sorry, I must have let my intuition lapse at Charm School.

You said it right. I guess I just listened wrong.

And then there was the pretzel maker who changed jobs because he got tired of making dough.

The cows that were flown in a spaceship? The herd shot 'round the world.

My Mama Said...

I felt like a rooster at an egg laying contest.

I've heard of tired blood, but this is ridiculous.

She arrived at her wits end after an incredibly short journey.

Sign on the wall of a traffic bureau; In 1980 there will be 200 million automobiles on the streets. If you want to cross the street, better do it now".

On Cape Cod there is a house named Psycottage and it has a small roadway behind it called Psycho-path.

When you stretch the truth, people usually can see through it.

Two pints make one cavort.

Sign in a maternity shop window. You should have danced all night.

She's built like a record player. 33 1/3, 45, 78.

Young boy, returning with his family from vacation, "Look, Daddy, you forgot to turn off the grass!"

Rooster, saying to the hens as he showed them an ostrich egg, "I am not disparaging, I am not criticizing, I am merely bringing to your attention what is being done elsewhere."

He always had both feet planted firmly in the air.

I only know the right answers when I get the right questions.

I am tempted to light the candle at both ends while I still have something to light it with.

If misery was snow, I'd be a blizzard!

My Mama Said...

The Pill: Something to be used in any conceivable circumstance.

On my good days, I look like a bale of hay in a watermelon patch.

Happiness depends on two assets, I've been told. Good health and a poor memory.

Butterflies? I've got bats and bald eagles in my stomach.

I've got all my marbles. They're just scattered a little bit.

Everything you say goes in one ear and out his mouth.

Her wit is so keen, so sharp, so firmly tempered you don't know your throat is cut until you laugh.

The greatest American composer; the tranquilizer.

The hand that rocks the cradle can still make a fist.

Some books could be improved if you moved the covers closer together.

Memory is what makes me wonder what it is that I forgot.

We have known each other from rocking horse to rocking chair.

I'm doing the work of three women. If I could find them, I'd hire them.

I swear, I've never seen baloney sliced so thin and piled so high in my life.

I wish some of the things I don't like were bad for me.

I would like each birthday to be a milestone, not a millstone.

My Mama Said...

I have an overriding desire to avoid the slightest effort.

I had more fun at boarding school than most kids had on purpose.

She shoots from the lip!

When you receive your hospital bill you will know why doctors wear masks in the operating room.

My house is furnished in early twentieth century disaster.

The snake charmer who married the mortician; towels marked Hiss and Hearse.

Children are deductible but they can be very taxing.

Better an empty car than a loaded driver.

In that furnace known as romance, his pilot light has gone out.

A bird in hand is bad table manners.

I have the Columbus system of typing, - discover, then land.

I used to approach each day as if I had been shot out of a cannon.

Adult - A person who has stopped growing at both ends and is now growing in the middle.

It is probably the duty of anyone who finds anything remotely funny in all of this to share it with those of us who are less fortunate.

CHAPTER SIX
POTPOURRI

Clothes aren't important; its how you feel inside them. When you go shopping, don't buy a dress, buy a feeling.

It was as if she had wrapped up her life and put it on some forgotten shelf.

The only mathematical equation I know about anything is once enough.

There's an old Chinese saying; "You never bathe twice in the same river".

There is a yearning in the wind for winter, drifting off; a wistfulness for long, closed in evenings. Then out of the yearning wind it comes - a wisp of song in-the air, a shooting star, high tide at water's edge, laughter afar off, and behold, it is a warm spring night.

He was 100% incoherent, but you know he means what he says.

Are you looking for proof to strengthen your beliefs, or proof to confirm your doubts?

It was purely reflective talk, the way a chicken's body sometimes keeps walking around after it's head has been chopped off.

I may be foolish, but I'm not a fool - and there is a difference.

It was like a whole set of personalities, one inside the other like a nest of Chinese boxes, and when I made an effort to learn what

My Mama Said...

was in the boxes I only discovered more boxes, in a constant state of metamorphosis.

We were wearing silly hats, blowing horns, rushing about yet in all the strident madness there was no real gaiety.

This hospital which houses both the disease and sometimes it's cure; I have learned to read in the eyes of the doctors the sum and measure of mortality.

This knowledge has been constructed of stout fabric, discovered among the cluttered aisles and tinseled bargain of bargain counters of experience.

The sky is still spitting snow and the desolate landscape made me feel as if I were the last soul alive on a forgotten planet.

I kept talking simply because sound seemed more manageable than silence.

Everything is neat and in it's place - everything but me.

There are too many people in this town for anyone to need to be lonely. But sometimes the more people there are the lonelier you get. I wonder why?

She had a body conditioned by diet and used practically not at all.

I am an incurable, totally addicted gift giver.

He is the only person I know who can reminisce about the future.

People being so aggressively cheerful make me tired.

I am not ashamed of any feelings I ever had. Can you say the same?

My Mama Said...

I was reaching the point of ultimate calcification.

The ancient alchemy transmutes our greens into yellows, reds browns and golds. The master artist, with a broad brush, converts the woods, the mountains, the forests into a polychrome tapestry and autumn paints herself in seductive colors and flaunts her multi-colored skirts in the abandon of the wind. Already the down-drifting leaves are settling like small sailcrafts on the cold earth, swirling and eddying about. Nature destroys to perpetuate.

Take a word, fondle it, polish it and then put it into a sentence,

Our neighborhood is a pleasant world of humble homes and humble people; yards, porches, swings, railings and rocking chairs.

It is harder to conceal ignorance than to acquire knowledge.

Sometimes somebodys absence can be just as strong as their presence.

He spends too much time struggling with self invented problems.

If I don't clean this house soon it will probably be eligible for Federal Relief as a disaster area.

I just do not belong in that nut house of a city where you have to break your neck to see a star.

I sleep slow.

Most holidays are a day off, followed by an off day.

Oh, for the good old days when Uncle Sam lived within his income and without most of mine.

My Mama Said...

I hope our friendship can survive the eccentricities of our friends.

After all, we survive every moment - except the last one.

The whole day was a masterpiece of timeless melancholy.

Why must the test of everything lie in it's durability?

I'm tired of working my heart out to erase something that is indelible?

I'm afraid I will never cast my footprint in front of that theater in Hollywood.

I wish she could know the degree to which her today will shape her tomorrows.

A watch is a little trap where we try to catch eternity and segment it into fragments small enough to possess; only we never really do.

A fisherman doesn't roil the waters before he starts fishing.

She was smooth and hygienic, calm and trite - a tormented mannequin.

One minute she was breathing and the next she wasn't. It was just like you'd blow out a candle... Where did the flame go?

I'm never at a loss for words, but I don't always use the right ones.

One of the troubles with life is that you have to live it forward instead of backwards, you can't just shed it like shedding a skin.

The leaves sounded like a deck of cards being shuffled.

My Mama Said...

He is suffering from the ravages of prosperity.

I think sometimes virtue consists of insufficient temptation.

She lives up to her reputation of being a pebble in the shoe, and keeps happiness out of hand.

A small bird in a tree outside said something, and then shut up for the night.

It is possible for a human being to turn out all the lights in their soul as instantly as one flicks a switch on the wall.

There are few disguises harder to penetrate than the all enveloping cloak of simplicity.

Oh, the luxury of <u>time</u>.

Sometimes I pass a mirror and I look into it and ask, "Who is that woman?"

When you start measuring someone, measure them right. You make sure that you measure all the hills and valleys they have been through to get where they are now.

How can some people get through life without a drop of rain touching them and other people barely get out the door without the whole sky falling on them?

It's easy to take a wrong turn, but it's hard to get back on the freeway.

As long as people keep asking questions, there must be answers.

The motion of the fire set shadows jumping and gave the paintings on the wall life and movement.

My Mama Said...

How careless is autumn with her brush, painting her passionate pictures all over the place and taking no thought for cleaning up afterward.

I'm the sort of person on whom nothing is lost - nothing gets by me.

A broken dream is better than no dream at all.

Only those who do not try are failures.

His smile was as false and artificial as the paper roses on his desk.

Are all men alike – stamped out with the same cookie cutter?

"Cool" describes everything from Mae West to Hoover dam.

You cannot force the reason and consciences of all people into one mold.

Things even out... the more body weight you carry around, the less time you'll have to carry it.

Why don't people just enjoy what happens? Why must everything make sense or have a reason?

Why was I telling him all of this? Because he was a stranger and strangers listen attentively, smile politely, and get of at the next station, so to speak.

I know I am guilty of some pretty expert self deception.

Do you know what sometimes causes death? Futility. No more reason for one more heartbeat.

Billboards are visible pollution.

My Mama Said...

Some people have unexpected depths of self respect which may be pretty well submerged until someone hits too hard.

It's like Christmas. Everybody being very nice to everybody for just a little while, you know. But, it doesn't last. It's impermanent, and it shouldn't be.

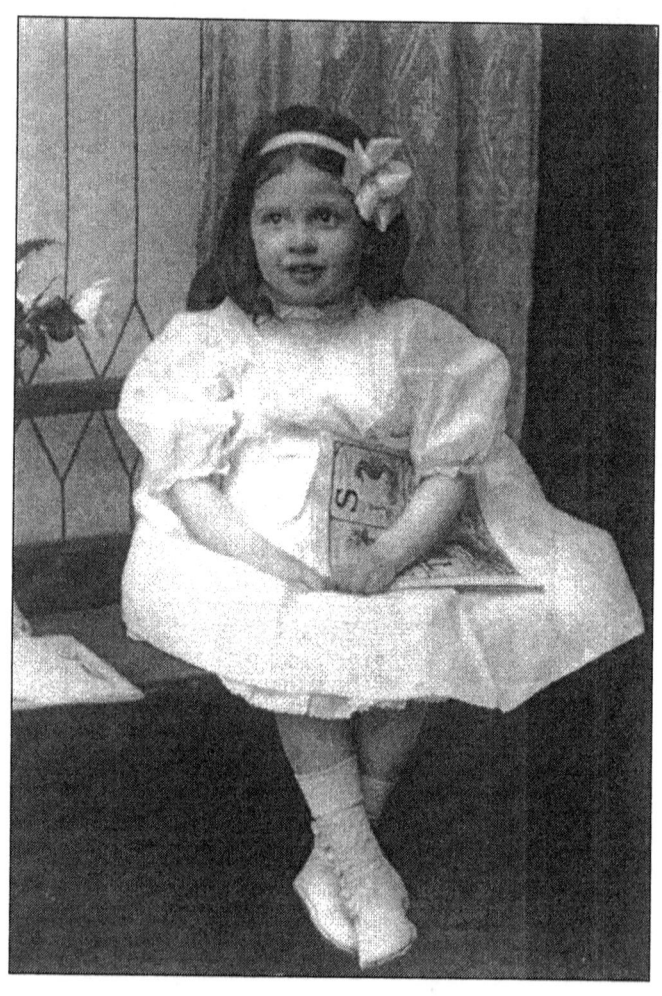

Mama at her 5th birthday party.

CHAPTER SEVEN
MY CHILDHOOD

I was buffeted about by instruction of interfering relatives, and to make matters worse and my road harder, the temper tantrums of my father. There was the indifference of who kept me. I needed to learn that adults could be people on whom children could depend; people who neither screamed at me or ignored me. I tried to retreat into a dream world where I could lose my acute fear of the real world in one not so frightening that I cope with. Maybe I was lucky I never quite made it into that dream world.

There is a staunchness, a stately charm about Bremo, where I spent summers as a child,

Great oaks arch the driveways creating tunnels of green, the gardens are-very old and satisfying and fragrant. Quite apart is the crass commercialism of the village which has the effrontery to call itself Bremo also.

Not only did my father want his own way, he wanted those who disagreed with him punished.

I was so little then, and so absolutely defenseless; so very complicated and so alone and I dreamed of a day when I would find somebody who would love me and would be with me forever.

I was an authority on homesickness, which was a little odd since I didn't have a home for six months at a time. I walked around as though part of me was missing. It was as if I was stranded in a silent movie with no subtitles.

My Mama Said...

My father always tried to nullify any creativity and ingenuity or inquisitiveness I ever had as a child. He wanted me only as a satellite. HIS satellite.

I was virtually robbed of the power of decision as a child. Under such circumstances, independence in later life was very hard. Time after time I have found it difficult to make decisions. When I finally married I expected to find romance, fun and freedom; instead I found I had merely exchanged the prison of girlhood for the prison of marriage, I had escaped a jailer father for a husband, immature to an extreme degree and our lack of communication was terrible. On rare occasions I tried to confide in him about my problems, but he was too preoccupied or disinterested to comprehend what I was trying to say. I took 90% of the blame for everything that went wrong, thinking of myself as "cold." Hah! There was nothing physically wrong with me. If we could have talked freely to each other, and more important, listened to one another, and most important of all, understood one another...

When I was a child I was too young to know what was frightening me.

As a little girl, I refused to accept my life as it was; I was always dreaming it could be different; I built defenses to protect me from frightening things - I attempted to escape unhappiness and loneliness. I was afraid. I was tense. Sometimes I panicked in a crowd. I was a very insecure and troubled little girl; sometimes withdrawn, sometimes outgoing. Both were defenses. I was afraid people wouldn't like me, and being loved was very important to me. I was old enough to have adult problems and too young to know how to handle them. I got batted around through the summer months like a ping pong ball; I learned to make adjustments fast. I fled many of the idiotic complexes that were so painstakingly affixed to me in my youth. If occasionally I had been permitted to show my feelings instead of having to work them out in the privacy of my own thoughts,

My Mama Said...

things would have been different. My father definitely never had any fears about inhibiting me.

It was always clear what my father wanted to emancipate me from, but it was never clear what he wanted to emancipate me for. I guess I have felt rejected all my life.

Sometime I would like to escape to that safe, charted world where the air smelled of chalk, the colors were paint box bright, the boundaries were the same all the time and all the ideas we could conceivably use were handed down to us, complete with punctuation, from a raised platform.

I used to pretend I could vanish. This little game of invisibility helped me feel like a little girl under her first Christmas tree.

I've lived inside a silky little cocoon all my life, like a blind little worm and now I am trying to push my way into the open. It isn't easy. Help me to climb over the barrier of my locked in self.

I got the fear of abandonment at a very early age, about six, perhaps earlier. My father would ask me what I would do if he left me and every time he left the house I'd fear that he would never come back and at the same time wish he never would. It was a frightening experience; sometimes I'd be filled with real panic. Nothing reassured me. My loyalties were terribly torn. I felt insecure and apprehensive.

When I was a child it seemed that whenever I had a good impulse I got punished.

Our teacher used to fix us with that Dead Sea gaze.

I come from a home - several homes! which might be euphemistically have been described as "underprivileged."

My Mama Said...

I was raised on prunes and proverbs.

That broken child had been sent away to boarding school and in that small, private institute had healed and found her way, emerging whole and unshaken on the far side of adolescence.

The very cruel can sometimes be very gentle. I looked forward to those charades of gentlemen, until I discovered that was all they were - charades.

Oh for those lovely, irresponsible days of youth.

Adolescence - the time of life that comes in with a pimple and goes out with a beard.
Do you remember the fears, and Sears, and tears?

That was before I had built the high wall around me. Only once did I climb to the top and look over but what I saw sent me toppling back into the darkness again.

She hovered on the fringe of things, reluctant, detached. She had been afraid to go to sleep at night because she didn't know where she went.

By the calendar I was ten; immersed in a fog that children of that age carry invisibility like a cloak you can put around you when confronted by grown folks.

I was supposed to be gently bred, gently reared and safe from all alarms.

I don't know how many times I moved, but each time the small ballast of hopes and plans I had collected were thrown overboard and everyone I had learned to know was left behind.

I believed in God; I served in His name. I hoped for a future life in heaven. But this brought me no comfort. I could not feel secure

My Mama Said...

with a God who seemed to be more tyrant than father. Especially since I knew a father who was a tyrant.

I never had a mother to kiss me or rock me or tuck me in, or show me how to make cookies; or a father to tell me he was proud of me, or that was the best little girl in the world. I took what I could find; every time anyone would be kind to me I adored them secretly.

Once I played an orphan child without a home in one of the plays at school - rarely has art imitated life quite so close to home, and when I cried real tears they marveled at what a good actress I was. And I wasn't even acting.

We were sent to a school with emotionally disturbed teachers.

In an estate closing I received some pages from my family history, and also the letters from my mother to my father so long ago. Those pages, like moth wings neatly powdered and folded closed had survived. No rain had touched it; no sunlight had bleached it. There it was, it lay upon my palm. What had she written? I opened it for now I had to know - I opened it, read it, and then I wept. A message from my mother to my father - yes, and even to me to some far distant me. Did she know that some day, I too would read it all? From the young mother to the baby - now grown old.

At Grace Street in Richmond, when I was small, I still remember the "thing in the closet." When I was put to bed for a nap in the daytime with shades drawn I would see it. Only a hat on a shelf and a coat on a hanger. I'm sure now, but then it terrified me. I was certain it would move. I screamed and begged my aunts to close the closet door, and they wouldn't. Why?

I was constantly plagued by the notion that my father would some day go away and leave me, and that anxiety, combined with the desperate hope that he would do just that made for a terribly

My Mama Said...

mixed up child. Nobody tried to help me with my emotional problems. In fact I don't suppose anybody ever knew that I had any.

In school-we would mouth whatever we thought our teachers wanted to hear. We were part of a system which rewarded us for obedience and punished us for individual initiative.

As a child, I had a loneliness which nothing and no one seemed able to relieve.

I never learned to walk: I went right from crawling to running...

I was belonging to nobody, wondering about the future, and losing myself inch by inch.

My Mama Said...

Now you have met my mama. I hope you liked her. She would have liked you the very moment she met you. I don't remember her saying anything bad about anyone. If she didn't approve of someone, she would keep quiet. I remember her saying, "if you can't say something nice about someone, don't say anything at all."

Mama's old typewriter with some of her writings in it.

About the Author

I was born in Charlottesville, Virginia, in the Great Depression. The date was September 6, 1929. We were like other families and didn't have much money at that time. I can remember five-cent loaves of bread, repainted old toys for Christmas, hobos that came to the house to work for food, all the things that the Depression produced.

I can remember the Roosevelt speech when he said, "the only thing we have to fear is fear itself." I can remember President Roosevelt coming down Monticello Road by our house while we waved flags and he waved at us. Mama had walked to town to buy them for us. My mama was always a big influence on my life. I can remember that my mama loved all of her children very much. She had not had a decent childhood and she was resolved to make our childhood as happy as possible.

I entered the United States Navy in 1947. I stayed three years in the navy and while in the navy developed my voice (I was in the Thousand Voice Choir at Great Lakes Training Center while I was there). In 1949 I was honorably discharged from the navy and wherever I could, I would be an entertainer. I still am in various theater guilds and sing for church and in Lion's Club shows whenever it is possible. Whenever I find someone with great talent, I encourage him, and if he is a child I encourage his mother to do something with that talent. I have helped children who went on to be in shows on Broadway in New York. I love entertaining.

I re-entered the service, this time the United States Air Force, in 1955 and stayed until I had twenty-two years' service. I then became a schoolteacher in Myrtle Beach, South Carolina. In 1986, our family dissolved and my son and I came back to Charlottesville and I bought back the house I had lived in since I was four years old. So when I came home, I really *came home*. I am retired now and have time to entertain, write poetry, do this book and also do whatever I wish. I worked hard for retirement and am enjoying whatever time I have left.

Lee Easton, Jr.

www.ingramcontent.com/pod-product-compliance
Lightning Source LLC
Chambersburg PA
CBHW071142090426
42736CB00012B/2200